To Carl
from Annemarie
October 15, 1943.

THE MANGROVE COAST

The Story of the West Coast of Florida

THE MANGROVE

COAST THE STORY OF

THE WEST COAST OF FLORIDA

BY KARL A. BICKEL

PHOTOGRAPHS BY WALKER EVANS

COWARD-McCANN, INC. *NEW YORK*

Designed by Robert Josephy

MANUFACTURED IN THE UNITED STATES OF AMERICA

TO HELEN MADIRA BICKEL

CONTENTS

viii   *Contents*

THE MANGROVE COAST

The Story of the West Coast of Florida

CHAPTER I

SAND IN YOUR SHOES

SOUTH FLORIDA is only a child as geologists count the years—a mere forty-five million years old, and still changing. Only yesterday, within the last twenty-five thousand years that is, the land level at Miami has risen six feet, tipping toward the northeast, and farther north and west it has sagged thirty. Variety and uncertainty are in the map of the Mangrove Coast, a name entirely arbitrary for that stretch of the west coast of Florida along the Gulf of Mexico from Ancolote Anchorage to Sanibel Key and then tapering off from Sanibel southward to the distant mouth of the Shark. The coast is more or less than its name—sediment, deposited skeletons of a hundred kinds of dead and gone marine life, Tampa limestone, marl, muck and peat. Coral unquestionably did its bit, and beautiful branching clumps of it are common finds on the beaches after heavy storms, but the mangrove, the sea grape and the cedar, far more than coral, built the land that lies along the miles and miles of snow white sand. The three brothers in the Mangrove

3

family, Red, Blackie and Whitey are the dominant construction crew all along the coast. Red is the advance guard of the family. The red mangrove races out across the glistening mud of an inviting flat and lays the preliminary bed of root wall. Afterwards the black and the white mangrove follow and build up, through the bent and twisted pattern of roots, a solid bed of matted shoots which, in their turn, gather up the sand, soil and seeds which set the coast and give it strength to resist the slap and bang of the long rollers from the gulf. Once started, the mangrove with its clutching roots scuttles along on ungainly legs that reach down through the sweep of the tide and through the mud and marl to secure firm grasp upon the bottom. Its gangly branches are soon encrusted with the "coon oyster," which in low water looks like dripping festoons of old and raveled rope. The mangrove's leaves are dark green and shiny, and sprinkled among them throughout the entire year are small pale yellow blossoms. In the north the mangrove rarely grows over twenty feet high and looks like a great bush rather than a tree, and despite its power against the wind and wave is an easy victim of the frost. As accumulation of sand and soil goes on the mangroves' work is assisted by the air plants and orchids which roost among its branches. Then comes the red cedar, the strangler fig and the saw grass. In the north the sabal palm will edge in. Farther south the sabal is likely to be joined by a leaning cocoa-palm. Below Sanibel and Everglades City in the region of the Shark the great wall of mangrove, made up of amazing trees, sometimes passing eighty feet in height, something to be seen nowhere else in all the world, form a deep green palisade along the shore. Behind it lie the mysterious depths of the Florida Labyrinth which has yet to be fully explored. Within the Labyrinth grows the great terrestrial orchid, tall-stemmed with splendid spreading pink flowers, often to be seen broken and mangled, floating on the waters but still beckoning to some fortunate botanist knowing himself to be the first to see it growing in its natural state. Here in the Labyrinth is the legendary lair of Buster Farrell's sixty-foot sea serpent. Along this shore in the mad tangle of the mangrove roots the wild dillies and the soap berry grow and close to the warm sands of the gleaming beach are thousands upon thousands of dwarf cacti. Farther south the land is so young its age is but "a tick of time." To the north over the centuries the accumulations of muck and marl have been far greater. Four thousand feet below the courthouse square in Tampa the foundation rocks of Florida are said to exist. But the average tourist passes geology by. He looks with today's eyes at today's sights. He cares little how much is in the coast and thinks less about the mangrove.

His eyes rest on the sponge markets that make Tarpon Springs as colorful as the old Aegean. The little boats with blue and russet sails; bronzed sponge fishers speaking Greek, Spanish and English; the millions of sea shells;

the swaying tendrils of the purple sea plum and the deli-
cate lacelike intricacies of the sea fan delight him.
Branching coral there is too, bone white and infinitely
various in design. And after a heavy sea, a writhing line
of dull green kelp tangled with oddly contorted seaweed
in brilliant white, orange and scarlet trims the coast.
Castled in the kelp are jutting-eyed defiant little crabs,
a world of inch-high devils. Poke at the kelp with your
stick or toe and the crabs will instantly swarm out of
the deep green recesses of the seaweed and with desperate bravery stand their ground, defiantly waving
their tiny, futile claws.

On such days, too, after a storm, thousands of sand-
pipers, sometimes herded by a big Wilson snipe, march
back and forth along the beach at Sarasota advancing, re-
treating with the waves, and devouring the little crabs
and coquinas.

The sunsets off Cap d'Antibes, off the atolls of the
South Seas, the sunsets that spill raw reds and orange
on the gaunt beaches of Lower California are worth
traveling far to see. On the Mangrove Coast the sun goes
down with a calm serenity all its own and special un-
stinted pouring out of color on the glistening sand. In
the spring it takes but sixty seconds for the great orange
ball to slip from sight from the time it first touches the
level line of the far horizon until the last tip of its golden
circumference disappears. It is a favorite trick of the old-
timers, standing on the beach in the evening, to make

wagers with the newcomers on the time consumed. It
seems much longer. As the sun fades the evening wears
an orchid veil like no other sunset in the world.

The coast is calm. But it is a strand littered with great
associations. No bastions, no cloistered missions, no
monuments to imperial history embellish it. But many
great names have passed its way, and though nothing
greets the eye, legend is abounding. Vespucci, Juan
Ponce de Leon, Diego Miruelo, Cordova, Francisco
Garay, Narváez, Cabeza de Vaca, Juan de Anasco, de
Soto and the martyred Padre Cancer all saw this coast
on their journeys four centuries ago. They sought, they
said, to expand God's kingdom and their own, and, not
altogether as an afterthought, to find gold. Some slipped
by into the early morning Gulf horizon; others disappeared in long, thin lines into the green darkness of the
palmettoes and the bearded live oaks never to return.
The few who might have stayed along the coast and
planted banners were driven away by the fighting Timucans. Three centuries were to pass before white men
obtained any permanent foothold on the Mangrove
Coast. But no coast once sighted, or even heard of, is
ever unexplored. If no white men in those centuries
came to conquer and to stay, they still held it on their
charts, Le Moyne's great map and that of Johannes
Schoner and the highly colored ones from the presses of
old Abraham Ortelius, Peter Goos and Gerard Mercator.

Maps are hard and fast, definite down to minutes and

degrees, but coasts, by themselves, are illusory things. The Mangrove Coast has its place with those other opiates of the map tasters who accept poetry and fantasy where your worried navigator wants longitude and latitude and great exactitude in fathoms. The China Coast, the Gold Coast, the Ivory Coast, the Cote d'Azur are real and definite places yet their boundaries are never really fixed; international conferences and high statesmanship can never quite define them. They are believed—they are governed by men's fancy. The China Coast, drawn by one map maker to include the west as far as Singapore, by another as reaching north to absorb Kamchatka, and by some other narrowed down to label only the shore from Hong Kong to the green and purple hills of Shan-i-Gwan is such a coast of story. It is much the same with them all. Wherefore in the midst of dreams about the Mangrove Coast, its leaping tarpon and buried treasure, in spite of a fondness for faded Spanish maps in Havana Museums, who writes about the West Coast of Florida must pull himself up short. In Drake's day a returned traveler could get away with the vaguest of directions —a wave of the hand toward the Western Sea and a tankard drunk to the "Western Isles." In these days of road signs, traffic officers and gas station sectional maps, people want to know the route, the station and the mile. With a hundred and twenty horse power under the hood, Harold Ickes peeping over the shoulder, and only three weeks clear of the office, a few substantial travel facts

are in order. One cannot moon about the Mangrove
Coast; nor even copyright the name without a lot of
argument with Chambers of Commerce from Perdido
River to Barnes Sound. Most of these will hold out for
an imaginary line just north of Port Richey, and some
will stick for cutting off at Sanibel Key, off Punta Rassa
passage, where—some say and others deny—old Ponce
de Leon received his death wound. Sanibel would have
to be included along with Gasparilla, La Costa and Captiva. It was on Captiva, say the believers of the legend
of the pirate Gasparilla, that the old buccaneer kept his
harem—hence the name. But no fragile bones or bits
of jewelry have ever been discovered there. This lovely
string of keys frames Charlotte Harbor and protects it
from the high rolling seas of the Gulf when the north-
ers come sweeping down in February. Fort Myers is
almost eighteen miles up the wide Caloosahatchee.
"Hatchee" is the Seminole word for river. On some of
the old Spanish maps the river is named the Carlos but
the "r" wore badly and both Seminole and settler soon
found it easier just to drop it. The stimulant of the Seminole wars, which founded so many Florida towns, established Fort Myers and the location of a Union battalion there during the Civil War further accounted for its
growth. In 1859 a South Carolina planter made extensive
plans for developing an American coconut plantation
at Fort Myers but he left with the firing on Fort Sumter
and there are still no commercial coconut plantations

at Fort Myers. Edison discovered the coast in the early
'Eighties, slumbering in its somnolent January sun, and
built a home and erected a laboratory there. Enthusiastic, he offered in 1887 to provide Fort Myers with
electric power for the three winter months entirely without charge, but the easygoing citizenry, quite satisfied
with candles and kerosene, said the cost of the erection
of the pole line was excessive so the project died. Edison experimented here with the use of bamboo as the
filament for the light bulb. The Duke of Sutherland was
a frequent visitor. He would leave his large land holdings north of St. Petersburg to sail south in his big yacht,
the *Sans Peur,* and call in state upon the inventor, at-
tended by four kilted pipers, tootling their heads off as
they followed the Duke from his tender up the palm-
lined streets. Much later Henry Ford and Harvey Fire-
stone came to settle on estates adjoining the Edison
property. Out of this group of neighbors grew Edison's
experiments to find a native source for the commercial
production of rubber.

For over five years Edison experimented with great
numbers of Florida weeds and plants in an effort to find
an acceptable substitute for the rubber trees of Malaya
and the Amazon as a domestic source of supply. He
finally settled upon the common goldenrod as the most
promising. During the latter years of his life, he devoted
many weeks of each winter season to his experiments
with it in his little green laboratory at Fort Myers. He

succeeded in extracting sound commercial rubber, but the cost of production from the goldenrod as against the cost of Malayan rubber seemed to be an insurmountable obstacle. Now, however, the sharp and breathless demands of war make little of peacetime costs. Goldenrod, which can be produced in Florida in enormous amounts within the space of a few weeks, is again looming up in the laboratories as a possible answer to a wartime emergency.

Fort Myers is unique. There are those who say it is no part of these United States at all. It is a suburb of Rio or Bombay, a fragment of Manila, a bit of old Panama, a truly tropical place, too tropical really, to be counted on the Mangrove Coast. Under its mile-long avenue of royal palms Fort Myers is not recognizable botanically as a part of the continental America. It might easily be an island, as Key West is, or a thousand miles nearer the equator, spread along Capricorn. Those who discount their eyes and claim Fort Myers for America point out that one can walk from Chicago to Fort Myers without crossing water more extensive than bridged stream. But they all admit that the journey from North Clark street is infinitely longer than the registered miles in the AAA map. Only the sky-reaching royals, the sapodillas, the mamee, and the clustered coconuts can tell you how utterly far we must have come.

Leave it at that. The tropics brush the Mangrove Coast but do not overwhelm it. The horticultural jour-

nals describe it as subtropical, which means that all fifteen native Florida palms grow there, and also the coconut and the lovely *Cocos plumosa*, a Brazilian émigré
which combines the glories of the royal with the coconut and is as sturdy and frost-resistant as the native
cabbage. Its feathery fronds float in the slightest breeze,
and to many its straight and slender trunk, the color of
old discolored ivory, has far more charm than the gray
white cement of the columns of the royal palm. Rows
of them can be seen in all the newer cities. The planning
experts use them to displace the rougher lustier Wash-
ingtonia. Talk of palms like talk of coasts runs on; there
is romance in the some two hundred varieties from Africa, Asia and Europe which have come to be natural-
ized citizens, beautiful, flourishing, bearing fruit in what
was once the New World. The native cabbage palm, the
slash pine, the three oaks, water oak, laurel oak and live
oak, the masterful and fertile mangrove, red, white and
black, the stark mysterious cypress are there in groves,
with here and there the giant flowering magnolia and
its cousin, the bay tree. The Chinese lacquer red of the
early swamp maple, the gray of Spanish moss, air plants
and native orchids, mottled, or red, or yellow, some deli-
cate as little bubbles, some so old that four strong men
can scarcely lift them—all these flourish on that coast.
Stand on the beach and look to sea. You will see crea-
tures as strange as the trees and plants—the rare and
lonely manatee, the great sea turtles, the slowly turning

dolphin, the flashing tarpon and the king. Then the old tales begin to take shape, tales of Spanish cavaliers, and smuggled drugs and Chinamen, of the wrecks when the bitter lash of the northwester has struck the coast. The sun is setting. Look about you. The saying goes that if you once get the sand of the Coast in your shoes, you will itch forever after with the longing to return to bury your toes in the sand of this shore, to smell its morning winds, and gaze at its high blue sky.

CHAPTER 2

BEFORE THE SPANISH CAME

IN the pre-Columbian era and for the first two centuries after the coming of Ponce de Leon, Indians—but not the Seminoles—dominated the Mangrove Coast. Of the two basic Indian groups in Florida the northern, the Timucans, lived roughly north of a line running from Sarasota Bay to Cape Canaveral. South of it the Caloosas held the vast area between Cape Sable and Sarasota Bay. On the east they divided the Everglades with the Tequestas, a closely related tribe with whom, in matters of importance, the Caloosas usually acted in concert.

The precise origin of these Indians is unknown. They seem to have drifted in from the north and west, part of the great Mushkogee emigration from beyond the Mississippi, which some believe to have been forced by pressure from the expanding Aztecs. Others believe that both the Timucan and the Caloosa stock came from Central America and Yucatan. That is not improbable. Much in their social structure suggests both the Mayan and the Aztec. Undoubtedly over centuries the Florida

Indians were in constant contact with the Carib, the Siboney and Arawak Indians of the West Indies, from Cuba and the Bahamas, Haiti and the north coast of South America, too, perhaps. Their language contained so many Carib words that it is probable the West Indian Indians and the Florida Indians could communicate without difficulty.

The men and women of both tribes were tall, clean-cut people, of a light brown hue. The women were notably attractive to the early Spanish explorers. Their short skirts of closely woven Spanish moss had all the appearance, pliability and softness of fine wool, the Spaniards said. Le Moyne's pictures, made near St. Augustine in 1565, show the men as definitely taller than their French visitors. This appearance of height was added to by the way the men bound their hair upon a light structure of vegetable fiber another foot higher. Bernal Diaz, who came in contact with the Timucans near Tampa Bay in 1517, reported that they looked like giants. A mound opened on Longboat Key off Sarasota Bay revealed two male skeletons, one of which was seven feet long and the other was almost eight.

Both Timucans and the Caloosas were sedentary. Their permanent homes were fixed and they had fields for cultivation of corn, pumpkins, squash and tobacco. They had well-organized fisheries and certain rude industries. Their shell mounds, sprinkled thickly over the whole gulf region, are sound evidence of the enormous number of oysters they consumed. They ate turkey, deer, opossum and often smacked their lips over a succulent baked rattlesnake. On occasion, following an intertribal raid, there is a sinister touch in their diet. The breasts of young girls, it was said, were especially reserved for the chiefs.

Their social organization was well defined. Their chief assumed the prerogatives of royalty; a nobility furnished the tribe's councilors and a "common people" provided the warriors. The chief, his queen, and the greater nobles were borne on litters of rich design when they traveled from village to village. These litters were carried by a fourth social category, a curious, very numerous element, berdaches, neutral as to sex, who were held to certain restricted tasks, heavy burden-carrying among these. They were usually dressed as women, although otherwise apparently regarded as inferior men.

Against the Spanish the Timucans won a name from the first as desperately brave fighters, until diseases, caught from the white adversaries, decimated their numbers and despoiled their vigor. Where they were, the Spanish made little progress in colonization except at St. Augustine. On the Mangrove Coast, after a few feeble efforts, the Spanish gave up hope of conquering them by force or even through the establishment of missions.

We know little of their tribal contacts, save with each other, and their concepts of commerce. The wide ranging Cabeza de Vaca, describing the life of the northern Gulf Coast Indians, who were probably Creeks in origin, pictures a surprisingly large play of intertribal trade from group to group into the far north and west. The evidence of contact with the people of the West Indies comes largely from the artifacts from the mounds; pottery and gold ornaments. But the record reports a Spanish-speaking, Spanish-hating Indian among those who appeared off the Gulf Coast with a squadron of attacking canoes against Ponce de Leon's fleet in 1513. This Indian told the surprised Spaniards, who had assumed they were traveling waters no white man had ever sailed before, that he came from Hispaniola (Haiti). The incident indicates sufficiently that visits were not infrequent.

Indians in almost all of the West Indian islands told Columbus of the great island to the north. Evidence from the mounds speaks even more positively. Dr. Cushing's discoveries in the shell heaps on Marco Key indicate Mexican contacts, while the finding by M. J. Tallant of Manatee of a beautifully worked Mayan gold Sun God, creeping alligator, and necklace, in a mound north of the Manatee River tells the same story. M. J. Tallant's collection of pre-Spanish Indian pottery and metal objects provides plenty of testimony to prove the case. The dogs of the Caloosas, it has been noted, were strikingly similar to the dogs of Peru.

The Mayans were great traders. Their merchants, in huge trading canoes, visited ports from the Columbian

coast to as far north as Yucatan. Columbus saw one of
these boats on his last voyage off the coast of Nicaragua.
It was, he reported, almost a hundred feet long, with a
seven-foot beam and supported twenty-five paddlers, the
merchant and his family of seven. It carried a palm-
thatched deck house and numerous cooking pots; and,
stowed away fore and aft, was a cargo of goods consisting
of woven cotton cloth, copper implements and jars of
Mayan beer. There are many months in every year
when such a craft could easily work from Yucatan
to Cuba and from Cuba to Key West and the Florida
mainland. Obviously there was not a great trade between the Gulf Coast and the Mayan ports but this
was not because of the distance but simply because the
Florida Indians had so little of value, in Mayan eyes, to
offer in exchange. The Caloosas and Timucans could
offer roseate spoonbill feathers, parakeet skins, some
furs, and perhaps some copper. While Moore, Schu-
chert, Stone, Fewkes, Cushing and Hrdlicka, collectors
of early Florida artifacts, have pioneered among the
Florida mounds, and earnest Floridian students like Tallant of Manatee and Moore of Sarasota, have carefully
searched through the debris of many mounds, there are
still hundreds of mounds as yet untouched, and in those
mounds much more remains to be discovered. The large
mounds of Weedin's Island in St. Petersburg, the important mounds of Terra Ceia Island and Sneed's Island
near Bradenton; the mounds along the Myaaka and

on the countless keys south of Charlotte Harbor and around the mouth of the Shark, have yet to reveal all their shell-encrusted secrets. Unfortunately, many mounds are ruthlessly ripped open every year by men utterly ignorant of scientific practice or understanding, seeking relics for tourists or hoping to find gold. Mound digging is fast becoming one of the last of Florida's big game sports. Unless mounds are placed under state protection their messages for the historian and the scientist will be lost forever.

We know that the Mangrove Coast Indians were sun worshipers. The fine, high temple mound at Terra Ceia Island shows the long ramp coming up from the west to the top of the pyramid where the temple, facing eastward, once stood. De Soto's soldiers destroyed it in 1539. The Indian villages were built on a series of low mounds, generally flanking one higher mound upon which stood the house of the chief. The palm-thatched houses were large enough for several families to dwell under one roof. Some were even spacious enough to house upward of a hundred families. After the Spaniards came, the Timucans seem to have withdrawn from Sarasota and Tampa Bay northward. By 1612, when the region was visited by Lt. Rodriguez de Cartayo, all the Tampa Bay country was Caloosa territory and their great chief had his capital at Charlotte Harbor.

The annals of the Coast record that a plague of chicken pox swept over the whole Gulf country late in the seven-

teenth century. The Indians were as helpless against it
as if it had been smallpox. Some years later that eager
slave-raiding Englishman, Governor Moore of Georgia,
pressed deep into north central Florida, forcing the Timucans and Caloosas to give ground before the British
and their Creek allies. The Caloosas retreated into the
'Glades. In 1763, when the Spanish ceded Florida to
the British, many of the Caloosas emigrated to Cuba
to escape British rule. The rest hid themselves in the
Big Cypress country south and east of Fort Myers. A
few of the Caloosas are said to have been implicated
with the Seminoles in the attack upon Captain Harney's
trading post at Fort Myers in 1839 and the year after
in the massacre at Dr. Perrine's plantation on Indian Key.
In the smoke and flame of the destruction of the Perrine
plantation the Caloosas slip from the pages of history. Today, unless perhaps in the veins of some vagrant Seminole,
there is not a drop of Caloosa or Timucan blood in all
Florida.

CHAPTER 3

PONCE DE LEON DOES NOT LOOK
FOR A SPRING

JUAN PONCE DE LEON did not discover Florida on Easter Day. Nor was he looking for a spring. In fact, it is by no means certain that he was the discoverer of Florida at all. John Cabot in his memorable voyage in 1497 sailed south along the Atlantic Coast an undetermined distance. Certain historians, bearing important names, support the theory that the Genoese navigator for Henry VII reached the coast of northern Florida. If he did, he made no landing of importance and brought no information of value back with him.

The far more noted voyage of Amerigo Vespucci is more historically important to the Mangrove Coast. Amerigo is the gentleman for whom the geographer Waldseemuller later named the western hemisphere. He made, with a considerable degree of now understandable secrecy, four voyages to the New World, the first of them in 1498. Much contradictory ink from historians' pens has flowed over these four voyages. Doubts, insinuations, charges and counter-charges are in the long record. If

Amerigo's statements as to these explorations are true, he was in fact the real discoverer of the North American continent, and the first European to set eyes and feet upon the Coast, the discoverer of Florida as well as of America.

Vespucci sailed from Cadiz on May 10th, 1497, accompanied by Vicente Pinzon and Diaz Solis, co-executives and pilots, with a fleet of four caravels. Following Columbus' trail, they set out first for the Canary Islands and laid a direct course for the Indies. Pinzon is a name famous in the Spanish sea history of that period. The Pinzons largely financed Columbus, and two of that family sailed with the Magnificent Admiral on his first voyage. Amerigo Vespucci was in one of the ship chandlers' firms that helped outfit the second Columbian exploration. The collaborators had a competent seaman's knowledge of the Admiral's course. The fleet met fair weather. They reached the vicinity of Cape Honduras on the Central American coast—the first white men to lay eyes on the North American continental land mass—in thirty-seven days. Columbus took thirty-four to reach San Salvador, a good nine hundred miles to the east of Central America. Making frequent landings, engaging now and then in friendly trading and occasional skirmishes with the Indians, Vespucci rounded Yucatan, crossed the Gulf and touched the Mexican coast at Tampico and then, sailing always to the north and northeast, he skirted the Texas coast, passed the mouth of the Mississippi,

and in April, 1498, sailed south the entire length of the
Florida gulf coast, passing through the keys and into
Biscayne Bay toward the end of that month. Thence he
sailed north, captured two hundred Indian slaves, re-
crossed the Atlantic and arrived in Cadiz. He sold his
human cargo in mid-October of that year. That, in brief,
is the story of his first trip.

Stress is laid on several facts by those opposed to the
acceptance of the Vespucci voyage. No official recognition seems to have been given to the explorer upon his
return, despite the fact that he stated in his letter to the
Gonfalonier Pier Soderini of Florence in 1504 that he
sailed under the sanction of King Ferdinand of Castile.
Much is made of the fact that after landing in Cadiz in
October, 1498, he made no known report in writing on
his momentous discovery until six years later in his now
famous letter from Lisbon to the Gonfalonier. There
seems, too, to be some evidence that Vespucci may never
have left Spain at all during the period in which he has
stated the voyage was made. The entire voyage, with
or without the sanction of King Ferdinand, was clouded
with not a little taint of illegality. Yet no one can study
the famous Cantino map of the Caribbean area, published in 1502, eleven years prior to Ponce de Leon's
first exploration, and not be convinced that not only
had Florida been discovered but that its entire coast,
west and east, had been rather carefully examined.

Presumably the map was drawn from notes obtained

from Vespucci or from some one who made the voyage with him. The outstanding features of the Florida coast line are generally well indicated. The three important indentations along the Florida gulf coast—Tampa Bay, Charlotte Harbor and Ponce de Leon bay—are shown, and the long straight line of the Florida east coast is correctly presented. There were maps of Florida prepared a century later that were no more accurate than the Cantino map of 1502.

Under Columbus' agreements with the King and Queen of Spain he had a complete monopoly on the business of exploring the New World. Restive King Ferdinand undoubtedly was concerned with the broad sweep of the Columbian monopoly on New World exploration. The King was in a subordinate position as against the Queen's rights in this matter. The Queen was ardently supporting to the limit the royal contracts of the Very Magnificent Lord and Don Admiral. Again the slave angle to the story was "off the record." King Ferdinand had no sentimental squeamishness about enslaving heathen from the Indies. It was, he held, fine for their souls and their heavenly future and also very good business, but the Queen, at this time, was adamant in her opposition. The fact alone that Vespucci brought back over two hundred Indian slaves would make the trip something best hushed up.

Close upon his first trip, Vespucci made another for the same interests that financed his initial voyage. Obviously it was to the interests of his royal employer to keep the voyages secret, and while Vespucci was still in Spain, it was not tactful for him to publish any of his exploits—particularly to the Gonfalonier of Florence, a rival commercial center likely to back its merchants in competing exploration. The evidence that Vespucci may not actually have participated in the voyages at all is long and involved, too long to be even discussed in a brief review. One crowning bit of evidence there is in Vespucci's favor, seldom sufficiently emphasized. This one fact seems to place the exploration beyond all dispute. That is the recognition of the voyage by Columbus himself. The Great Admiral was a man of many sides, of moods and fantasies. But there can be no question as to his supreme position as a seaman, a geographer, an explorer, and, in his time, an authority on maritime adventure.

Columbus made his fourth and last voyage to the New World in 1502. It is interesting that the King, having been secretly in the slave-running business with Vespucci for almost four years, in his final instructions to the Admiral told him he "must not bring back slaves." The Queen's influence was still dominant. Columbus was obsessed with the vision of finding a new passage to Cinpango. He touched North America, for the first and only time, somewhat north of Panama, sailed south and then north to Cape Honduras. He found gold. He found pearls. Not poor unrefined gold but great slabs of pure ore, valued almost $400 to $600 per slab. He came into contact with a Mayan trading canoe, a hundred feet long, maintaining a crew of over thirty men and women, loaded with Mayan pottery, copper articles and cotton goods. On the verge of touching both the Mayan and the Aztec empires which later enriched Cortez and Alvarado, the Great Admiral ignored the appeal to his cupidity. He pressed on to find the passage. Failing, his ships worm-eaten, the rigging rotten, he struggled back to shipwreck and disaster before ever he reached Spain and the royal court. The Queen, the Admiral's always staunchest friend, was dead; his stock at court was low; men found his story wearisome. Much of the gold he had taken from the Central American coast had been lost on the Jamaican coast. The Mayan goods for which he had traded had vanished. He needed confirmation of his story, and support. In this hour Columbus turned to Amerigo Vespucci. Vespucci had sailed north from the very point at which Columbus had closed his northbound cruise, and knew the coast. He knew its people and could testify to its wealth. "Tell them," said the aged and ailing Admiral, fighting desperately against the court cabal who itched to get their fingers into the golden pie, "what you have seen and what I have seen." And Vespucci for some months acted as an employee of the old sea dog who had won for Spain a New World and for the world a New Era.

There was no question in the mind of the Great Ad-

miral. He accepted the fact of Vespucci's trip. Bitter
he may have been over the implied disloyalty to him
and his rights, in the King's permitting the Vespuccian
voyages to be made at all. But Columbus and his sons,
wise to the ins and outs of every Atlantic port in Spain,
knew the facts. And needing a witness, Columbus secured that one in Vespucci, the only explorer in all Spain
except himself who had ever charted a course from the
old continent to the new.

Vespucci *may* have been Florida's first European
visitor. Cabot may have sailed past the mouth of the
St. Johns. Illegal and unauthorized slave-hunting expeditions slipping out at night from Haitian or Porto Rican
Spanish colonial harbors, creeping through the Bahamas
to the Florida coast, there certainly must have been.
Rumor and report abounded as to the fact of the land
and even as to its contour and general shape. Later on
the Spanish government in formal decree laid claim to
Florida, asserting they had held the rights of discovery
since 1510, three years before Ponce de Leon saw the
shores of Florida.

The expedition of Juan Ponce stands out romantically
from its proper mold and setting. For centuries the year
in which he made the trip was reported as 1512. Not until earnest work on Spanish documents during the middle
years of the last century was it proved conclusively that
the voyage was made in 1513. The Easter Day discovery
legend dies hardest of all. Lowery in 1901 in his "Span-

ish Settlements," placed the date of Juan Ponce's landfall as April 2nd, 1513, and Frederick Davis, in his noteworthy study of the Juan Ponce explorations in the special Florida Historical Society supplement of 1935,
proved conclusively that Juan Ponce was almost four
hundred miles from the Florida coast on Easter Day.
Yet the legend, as well as the fantasy of the youth-
reviving spring, persists.

The log of the Juan Ponce voyages no longer exists.
The best account is that by the Spanish historian Herrera, writing eighty years after the event, and apparently
with the log before him, which gives the world the only
known detailed account of the famous Spaniard's adventures. A fighter of repute against the Moors, a member of Columbus' second expedition, a highly regarded
fighter against the Indians of Haiti and Porto Rico, and
later governor of Porto Rico, Juan Ponce was no amateur in New World affairs, when, due to a switch in
power in the factions that controlled the royal court
in Seville, he was deprived of his work as colonial governor.

"Thereupon," states the old chronicle, "Juan Ponce,
seeing himself rich, determined to do something by
which to gain honor and increase his estate." There was
plenty of news about the islands to the northward. The
Indians talked of Bimini. The legend of health-restoring
springs in the lands to the north was part of every In-

dian's stock of tales. Columbus had heard it. "The springs" were one of the current jokes along the water side. Other reports were more important and more credible: "gold in the lands to the north"—slaves to be taken —beautiful women; and perhaps more certain and alluring, spices and rare woods. So Juan Ponce made the weary journey back to Spain and to Burgos, where the court then stayed, and there argued, wrangled, drank and diced his way through all the obstacles and obstructions that encompass any man in every time who arrives in a capital seeking power and privilege. The King's consent was won. Juan received his patent. It was a relatively short and simple document. Gold, justice—high and low —the King's tenth and Juan Ponce's over-all percentage were handled with directness and clarity. Nothing was said about the souls of the Indians, but a good deal about the division of their bodies. The deed was signed, states the old manuscript still in existence in Seville, "at Burgos, February 23rd, 1512, by command of the King." It was sealed by that fine and staunch old friend of Columbus, the Bishop of Palencia. No reference was made in it in any place to the business of expanding the Kingdom of Christ.

Juan Ponce returned to Porto Rico and set about collecting his fleet and supplies. The following March he was ready to depart. He was slightly over fifty years of age, sound in bodily health, certainly no palsied seeker after aphrodisiacal beverages and a new lease on sexual life. His crew was made up of veterans of New World exploration and strife. He had three vessels. Of these only the *San Christoval* was of any size. He held his troop down to fighters and sailors. No priests were taken, no doctors and no savants. He needed no alchemist to show him gold. As for doctors there were always many in the crew who could render the rough and ready treatment that passed for marine hygiene in those days. The doctor Columbus took with him on his second voyage found himself overworked when the crew were attacked in mass by dysentery after eating wild native fruits. The doctor, feeling himself badly underpaid, appealed to Columbus for a raise. The best the Magnificent Admiral would promise was that he would write the Queen about it. Juan Ponce did not want to be bothered with any such details.

Ponce sailed from Porto Rico on March 3rd, 1513. The fleet did "eight leagues of a day's run" on the night of March 4th, thus proving that Juan Ponce was a night sailor and that he did not lay up, as some do, while cruising in barely explored waters. A league was approximately two and a half miles so the night's run netted about twenty-one miles. Obviously this was a short run. Davis, in his studies on Juan Ponce, estimates the fleet did about two miles an hour or around fifty miles per day. Others think this was a low average. Fifty miles every twenty-four hours for vessels of this class was

certainly not exceptional. There has been a great deal of
nonsense written about the size and unseaworthiness of
the sixteenth-century vessels which made the early trans-
Atlantic crossings. The old caravels and galleons were
pretty able seagoing concerns and with wind over their
tails they could make very fair time. They were not as
flexible as the modern schooner but they did achieve
some amazing voyages in good time and condition. The
vessels of the original Columbus fleet were selected by
Columbus and his partners, the Pinzon brothers of Palos.
They had no wide field for choice but they did not need
it. The three of them were probably the ablest navigators
in Europe, sea wise in every way. They picked the three
vessels, and by Columbus' express wish, selected small
ships, with light draft. The Columbian fleet made the
last leg of its first voyage, from the Canary Islands to
San Salvador, in thirty-four days. That's good sailing
today.

The caravel type was a long low-waisted, narrow-
beamed craft, with one over-all deck, three masts and
a high, three-decked house after and a smaller structure
in the bow. Often the caravels were lateen rigged. The
Santa Maria was so equipped until just before her departure when Columbus had her rerigged to square sails.
The *Santa Maria* was one hundred seventeen feet long
and ran about two hundred thirty tons. Juan Ponce's
boat was of about the same general character and size.
Boats of this class drew around eight feet, were handled

more easily than larger vessels and could be worked closer in to the shore, which is important in a voyage of discovery. They were faster, too. Columbus did as high as three hundred miles a day. He frequently did one hundred twenty miles. His average was slightly over ninety. It is hard to estimate exactly the speed of Juan Ponce's fleet because of the varying conditions under which it sailed. It is about eleven hundred miles from Porto Rico to latitude 30.08 on the Florida coast where Juan Ponce made his first landfall. The fleet was off Key Abaco on Easter Sunday, March 27th, something under four hundred miles from the Florida coast where he secured his landfall April 2nd, just six days later. That gives Juan Ponce an average of about fifty-five miles per day, which is probably pretty close to what the fleet actually accomplished.

Easter Sunday was March 27th and, as has been pointed out, Juan Ponce was off Key Abaco. Still sailing northwest, as straight as a homing pigeon, Ponce, six days after Easter, at noon, on April 2nd, made his landfall off the Florida coast. He was then, it is believed, about eighteen miles north of St. Augustine. He was never closer to that little community which now so well commercializes his name. Throughout most of the afternoon of that day he sailed slowly north, using the lead a greater part of the time and getting an average of nine fathoms. Uncounted billions of tons of water have heaved and rolled over that sandy beach since the bright April day four hundred and thirty odd years ago. The charts still make it nine fathoms and a bad spot for a skipper to be in who is on the lookout for a quick safe harbor. As he edged in closer to the beach, Herrera states, Juan gained the impression of a beautiful view and cool woodlands. It had been a long, hard trip from Porto Rico. The sun had beaten down relentlessly as only the Caribbean spring sun can. Juan Ponce and his men had no automatic ice machines nor perfumed oils to assuage their sunbaked backs and flaming noses. The tall pines, the close clustering leaves of the palmetto, the spreading live oaks with their silver beards of moss and the miles and miles of dark green mangrove must have beckoned to the men with promises of swift brooks, soft sward and deep, cool shade. That's what sailors think of, next to women and whisky, when they first come up to a new and untried coast from a burning tropic sea.

Sometime between that late afternoon arrival on April 2nd and the morning of April 8th, Ponce de Leon went ashore and took possession. If he made any ceremony of it, the affair must have been most simple. He had no priests for mass, no government officials, no historians. His right and title to the land was made active and vital by the mere fact of his arrival. Juan Ponce was no man for unnecessary display. The fleet was in need of fresh water for the butts and dry firewood for the galley, and this was secured. The water was of a brackish taste and slightly regarded. The Fountain of Youth story cropped up later as columnists' gossip. A glib and often interesting historian of sorts, one Peter Martyr, attached to the Spanish court, made a practice of writing chatty and informative news letters of the ins and outs of the Spanish court to a selected group of distinguished clients. One of these was the Bishop of Rome, and to him one day Peter Martyr wrote that in the gossip brought back from the New World was a truly good one, that among the newly discovered islands "there was one in which there is a continual spring of running water of such marvelous virtue, that the water, being drunk (perhaps with some diet), makes old men young again."

That was all.

But today, as in the sixteenth century, in Rome or in any man's town, that was news.

Juan Ponce never saw the mouth of the St. Johns river though he must have driven very close to it. Had he sailed north a little farther, perhaps if he had kept his course but another fifteen minutes, he would have freed his vision from the high-topped palms that hid the view of the river mouth from the south in those days and made the discovery. But he did not and soon turned south. His little vessels fought off the mystery of the Gulf Stream, the clawing fingers of which kept his ships from properly answering to the rudder and caused him great difficulties. In the end, after one slight battle with the Indians and a few days' stay in Biscayne Bay, near Miami, he sailed south into the mazes of the Florida keys. Beyond lay Tortugas, Espiritu Santo Bay, fair-faced, fierce Indians, a trickle of gold—and the shadow of Death itself. This he did not know. He sailed on.

CHAPTER 4

THE LADY BELCHED

THE fleet lay in the deep velvety darkness of the May night. There was a slight wind, scarcely a breeze, and the dark surface of the Gulf was hardly broken by occasional ruffles as the wind passed lightly over the surface. But the air was fresh and the man at the tiller felt that daylight was not far away. On the foremast a small light twinkled. Close to the tiller, another lantern hung. Now and again, as the caravel lazily lifted and rolled, a beam would strike the steersman's face as he bent over his gear, or reveal a raised arm and hand.

To the left the steersman could see pin pricks in the night, the lights of two smaller vessels. To the right on the sea's edge lay a sliver of gray and pink.

A door banged aft in the shadows that concealed the high three-decked castle of the caravel and immediately the solid stamp of booted feet was heard descending the companionway. A cloaked figure emerged.

"All well?" he asked curtly.

"Yes, my Lord, Juan Ponce. A calm night, the wind

from the east. The water shoaled two hours ago. We lie here until dawn."

"What does it make?"

"A trifle better than two fathoms. Hard sand on the bottom and grass also. We will see land with the sun."

The cloaked figure ascended to the top deck of the after castle.

Juan Ponce signed briefly to the watchman stationed on the top deck. He moved toward the rail looking eastward. He was joined a moment later by another figure, wrapped in a dark cape and likewise wearing a flat black beret over his head.

The vessel slowly rose and fell in the light swell.

"Buenos dias, General," said the newcomer.

"Buenos dias, de Alaminos."

"It looks like a good day," said Alaminos. He was plainly the younger and a sailor to his finger tips. He studied the widening flush of gray and pink to the east and sniffed as the offshore winds seemed to freshen.

"Land smell in that breeze," he remarked. "I doubt we are a league off. The watch reports no lights and has heard no surf. But we must be very close—almost too close. Two fathoms and a half is not enough by far on a ledge of coral."

"Where do you place us?" asked Ponce, shifting against the rail so that he might look directly at the other man.

"As you know," de Alaminos replied, "at noon yesterday we caught a fair sight. The sea was calm enough and the vessel steady. I made it about twenty-seven degrees. We have not had a better sight since we turned Tortugas and set for the north.

"But," de Alaminos continued, "one thing gravely puzzles me. In all my experience as a pilot in these New World waters, with the exception of the great northward currents that we met off Cabo de Corrientes, I have never found a vessel respond so slowly to the northeast. There is no reason for it. True, our vessels are foul with weeds. The wind has generally been from the southeast, which would give us a tendency to drift to the northwest. Yet, day after day, if my reckoning be right, we have made but a small part of the easting. I can find no trace of a current. Certainly," and the pilot shrugged in disgust, "nothing like we met off Cabo de Corrientes. Remember the day off the river you named La Cruz and set up the Cross? The brig could find no anchorage, and was swept from sight for over a day by that terrific current. Juan de Cosa, the cosmographer, will be glad to hear of that affair."

"Tell de Cosa nothing now," replied Juan Ponce de Leon a trifle curtly. "What we Spaniards know, we know. The beastly Portuguese are already causing trouble and the English and French both dream of stealing this land, if they can, or of cheating the King and his subjects of the contracted fruits of their labors. The fewer the charts, de Alaminos, the better our hard-won secrets are protected. If you keep more in your mind and less on charts, the greater and stronger will wax the fame of de Alaminos, the great pilot of the New World."

De Alaminos acknowledged both compliment and deft rebuke with a sweep of his hand.

"You are right, as always, my General. Only Diego Miruelo and I have really studied these waters, made soundings of value and noted the prevailing winds. Our reports in the archives at Santiago will some day be of value to Spain. I hope to you too, sir," he concluded.

To the east the dark rim of the shore showed against the lighter green of the gulf waters and the high pink and yellow flush that overcast the sky. The night was fading away. The wind had kicked up a slight swell and the choppy waves were lightly capped with foam. A gull swooped suddenly deckward, cutting its fall sharply and pulling up and leveling off between the masts with a hoarse cry of surprise. Overhead a long line of great golden-crested pelicans twisted their heads as they passed over, casting a solemn, almost sinister glance downward. The beach line had crept close and topping the solid masses of mangrove, live oak and palmetto reared the bone gray skeleton of a great pine, its warped and distorted limbs reaching upward in gigantic supplication as if the dying tree had stiffened in a last agony. The sun, topping the rim of green, shone brightly.

Juan Ponce looked at the pelicans. "I wonder," he said to de Alaminos, "if they always fly that way, in odd

numbers. Did you ever see an even-numbered flock?
Notice how each one follows every soar and dip of the
leader. What an admiral! De Alaminos, you think you
are a pilot. Learn from the pelican. When I am in Madrid I can get those fellows about the court to believe
anything I tell them about the New World, but they will
not believe my stories of the pelican. They credit the
tailed Indians of the southland, and the unicorn and the
mermaids—did you ever see a mermaid, de Alaminos?—
but birds like these they say cannot exist; it would be
ungodly. One old priest openly charged me with prop-
agating heathenish doctrine. He said there was nothing
in the Bible, and particularly nothing in the Garden of
Eden at all like the pelican. It could not exist."

"What did you tell him?"

"I told him that I knew that too, but that God had
made the pelican as the repository for the soul of Cain.
It could not have been in the Garden of Eden."

"I don't like the way the *San Christoval* is acting," said
Alaminos, suddenly becoming professional. "She's dragging a lot of weeds on her bottom—I'd like to beach her
and clean her up. The brig needs it too, but it can wait."

"Perhaps we should," said Ponce, absently. Then with
keener interest: "Look, that's a false coast. The real beach
line is beyond; what we are looking at are islets in front.
We will go north today, and if we see no hills or country
that appears to offer gold or metal, we will turn about
and tomorrow seek some harbor to the south of us. If

we find a shelving shore we can beach the *San Christoval*. The crew will like stretching their legs and a meal a day on land. We need wood and fresh water. We know nothing of this Florida. If no gold is there we must look over the natives and judge whether they would make fit laborers in San Juan or Spain. On the east coast the devil is in native hearts and bodies. They fought like furies."

He continued. "I want you to see to it that our men forward understand I want no trouble with the natives over women. This business of hunting encampments and chasing girls into the brush has got to be stopped. These Indians are sharp men, not Moors or Jews, and we are much too far from our base to take on unnecessary fighting. I've been fighting Caribs for years in San Juan and most of it was caused by women. It wrecked Don Cristobal Colon's first settlement at La Navidad in '92. It sets the old men on edge and the old women begin caterwauling all over the place. Anyhow, no fighting Indian makes a good field hand. I want to be free to look into this country. Don Cristobal thought there were cinnamon and other spices in Española. Not up to the grade though of what we get from Cinpango. Perhaps they have spices here."

"Perhaps, my Lord," de Alaminos replied with just a hint of a smile, "you might find the old Indian's spring. Remember, the sorcerer said that if you drank or bathed in it your youth would be strong again."

Ponce smiled. "I remember. Perhaps even the spring. But I would rather find a gold mine or a land where slaves could be gathered easily. The run is short from this coast to Española where good hands bring ready money at the dock. Yet a youth-restoring spring would not be bad at all, de Alaminos. To tell those wenched-out gallants at Court I could bring back their youth with baths in my spring, would be worth a million ducats a year with passage money thrown in. The king would have to use the whole royal navy to bring them over, so great would be the press. Bishops too. Might there be any truth in it?"

"Who knows?" mused de Alaminos. "The Indians have talked of it for years. To the north in the great island, they say in Bimini, there is a spring where the people go to drink and bathe and restore themselves to youth. Many in Don Cristobal's day believed in it. No one can say the contrary. Anything can happen if it be God's will.

"Let us look for it. Great springs there are in the New World. Do you remember Dona Isabel, wife of the San Juan governor's secretary? The new governor's party were blown badly off their course, and when the storm left them they were south of Cuba, near the islet Don Cristobal named Pinos. The food was so bad and the water so foul that the good lady was close to death from an agony of the stomach. But near the coast of Pinos a great spring was found by the sailors that gushed out

like a river. The water was veritably alive. Your tongue
touched it and the very skin snapped and stung. She
drank and within ten days her hurt was gone. She ate
all of everything and reached San Juan in more health
than when she was in Spain."

"Was she younger?" asked Juan Ponce eagerly.

"Not younger," replied de Alaminos, "at least they
did not say. But they did tell that if you drink well of
these waters after eating you belch most comfortably."

CHAPTER 5

AT TAMPA BAY

SOUTH of Biscayne Bay Juan Ponce took his fleet, twisting in and out among the keys, proceeding cautiously as befits travel in waters regarded as dangerous even today. On Sunday, the day of the Feast of the Holy Spirit, they "ran along the coast of rocky islets ten leagues," which is distinctly slow going. Juan Ponce continued west, sailing as far as Dry Tortugas. On or about May 18th he laid his course sharply to the north and northeast. "They continued sailing," says Herrera, "sometimes to the north and at other times to the northeast until the twenty-third of May (six days) and on the twenty-fourth they ran along the coast to the south (not trying to see if it was mainland) and as far as some islets that extended out into the sea. And because it appeared that there was an entrance between them and the coast for the ships, in order to take on water and firewood they stayed there until the third of June, and careened one vessel called the *San Christoval.*"

On that brief statement rests the whole case as to

44

where Juan Ponce made his gulf coast landing. He remained on and about this island for almost twelve days. It was here he made most contact with the Florida Indians. He found low-grade gold and traded for it. Likewise he found a fertile land; great trees fit for shipbuilding, and a large and fierce Indian population. Though the days he spent on the island were marred by constant bickering and some outright fighting with the Indians, Ponce was never able to erase the memories of it from his mind. For eight long years the picture remained and called him back. He went again in 1521 for the best organized colonizing effort yet attempted by the Spanish in the New World. But time had only made the anger of the Timucans against the Spaniards higher and hotter. Almost as they landed—close, it is believed, to his former anchorage—his expedition ran into heavy Indian fighting. Ponce was wounded in the side by an arrow tipped with fish bone, and died shortly after in the newly founded city of Havana. But all of that was still to come on that day in early June of 1513.

For six days, "sometimes to the north and at other times to the northeast," Juan Ponce sailed on into the untracked waters of the gulf. The weight of historical opinion is committed to the theory that Juan Ponce in his north-northeastward course most probably reached the waters near Charlotte Harbor. Davis, close student of the Herrera record and the Florida explorations of Ponce de Leon, is strongly of the opinion that the ex-

plorer went no farther north than the 27th parallel, to
a point off the little city of Englewood, thirty miles
south of Sarasota. From here he sailed south on May
24th, Davis believes, and then turned eastward along
Sanibel Island beach, then north, threading the tricky
shoals of San Carlos Bay to the southwest of Fisherman's Key, keeping well west of St. James Point on
Pine Island, then heading north over the shallows of
Pine Island Sound into the safe depths of Charlotte Harbor. Somewhere along the broad reaches of the Sound,
Juan Ponce found anchorage, perhaps on the northeast-
ern shore of Pine Island. The charts give it in spots a
depth of eight feet. If the theory of the Charlotte Harbor
landing be accepted, it is surprising that historians do
not have Juan Ponce enter through the Boca Grande
channel just south of Gasparilla Island. This was, and
still is, the best natural channel into Charlotte Harbor.
It is easily noted, both by a slight discoloration of the
water and the conformation of the shore line. Prudy's
chart of these waters for 1823—many years before any
government work was done on the west Florida coast—
clearly shows a deep natural channel through Boca
Grande, and definitely indicates the San Carlos Bay
channel as uncertain and shallow. If Juan Ponce entered
Charlotte Harbor from the north, the Boca Grande
would be his natural entrance, and he would have anchored on the east side of Gasparilla Island, much
as did the schooner crews of later years who discovered

the natural advantages of the Boca Grande, and the deep
water on the east side of the Island. Here the water
ranges from twelve to fourteen feet, shelving off to seven
feet close in, and this would be just the spot to careen
a vessel of the *San Christoval's* size. If Juan Ponce did
negotiate the narrows of San Carlos Bay, and, kept on
northeast to Punta Rassa, he worked his fleet into the
natural harbor later so extensively used by Cuban
schooners carrying cattle from the Caloosahatchee River
cattle ranches. If the Pine Island landing is to be regarded as essential to support of the theory of Juan
Ponce's discovery of Charlotte Harbor, it would seem
from the charts that the most likely spot for the landing was on the south side of the key, between St. James
Point and St. James City where eight to ten feet is given
on the charts.

Certainly Charlotte Harbor is northeast of Dry Tortugas. It would have been quite possible for Juan Ponce
to have made the journey, as many historians believe.
Herrera reports that Juan Ponce's men, in conversation
with the Indians, learned that the Chief's name was Carlos. The Indians whom the Spaniards later termed the
Carlos Indians lived there. If not much weight can be
placed on that bit of evidence, it is because Spanish trans-
literation of Indian names was not very accurate at
any time, and particularly in the early years of the sixteenth century, and all sailors are inclined to approxi-
mate the native sounds by anything that roughly cor-

responds to their own language, and let it go at that. Also, in some curious manner (which reveals the Indian intelligence of the period), the Florida Indians had already gained a slight knowledge of Spanish words through contacts with the Cuban Carib Indians. Carlos, they knew, was the Spanish word for their great chief. It would not be surprising if, when the Caloosa Indians indicated their chief, they referred to him in some guttural approximation of "Carlos" hoping to make the strangers understand.

Swinging about Dry Tortugas on May 18th, setting his course to the north and to the northeast, then north again and east, there were two possible points of arrival, two harbors that closely fit the Herrera description of Ponce's landing. One is Charlotte Harbor. The other is Tampa Bay. Both face the southwest. Both are magnificent bodies of inland water, potentially two of the finest harbors in the world. Both are screened from the dancing waves of the gulf by long lines of narrow keys; both figure largely in the romantic history of later Spanish exploration.

At this point, to an investigator of Juan Ponce's probable landing spot, the speed of his fleet becomes important. When we left the little armada off the east coast of Florida it was averaging around fifty-five miles per day. Over six weeks have passed. Juan Ponce's vessels are wooden, and have accumulated grass. We know this was true because Ponce's first act after finding a safe anchorage on the Coast was to careen the *San Christoval* and clean the weeds and barnacles off the bottom. Such a growth would have a tendency to slow up the fleet. It is hard to say how much, but gulf coast fishermen who weekly work the Juan Ponce course from Tortugas to Tampa Bay estimate out of their own experience that it might amount to as much as ten miles per day. This would reduce the fleet's daily run to forty-five miles.

Six days of sailing north-northeast of Dry Tortugas would bring the fleet some two hundred seventy miles to the northeast of Dry Tortugas and almost fifty miles inland, definitely no place for Juan Ponce's fleet. Other factors must be counted in. One of these is the fact that during the month of May the prevailing wind is out of the southeast, and another is the existence of a slight but well defined northwestward current along the gulf coast. Striking the shallows off southwestern Florida, it darts north and northwest, and in springtime, when the southeasterly wind is dominant, it is always strong. Fishermen and officials of the Coast Guard estimate that the strength of the current is such that it would carry wooden sailing vessels of the caravel type better than a half mile an hour to the northwest and that this, in conjunction with a wind from the southeast, might have given a very definite northwestward tendency to Ponce's fleet. It is interesting that Herrera notes that the fleet sailed to the north and then "at other times" to the northeast, indicating that they frequently returned to the north course and then, finding themselves trending to the northwest more strongly than they expected, reverted to the northeast, only to be puzzled again by their failure to keep the northeast course as planned. Of course the existence of this current was unknown to the Spanish. In fact, it has very little recognition to this day. Yet it exists, and it was a real element in shaping Juan Ponce's northern course.

It is one hundred sixty-five miles from Dry Tortugas to the intersection of the 27th parallel and the Florida coast, a few miles north of Englewood in Sarasota County. Granting that Juan Ponce sailed a much more definite northeastward course than is justified by Herrera's brief description, and allowing also for a deflection in the course of the vessels to the northwest of twelve miles per day due to the current, Juan Ponce should have made his Englewood landfall some time on the fourth day out from Dry Tortugas.

Yet he sailed north and northeast for six days. *What became of the remaining two days?* On the basis of a forty-five miles per day average sailing, making allowance for the northwestward drift of the current, at the end of six days Juan Ponce would be somewhere south of New Point Richey off Anclote Key. Then, states Herrera, without landing he sailed southward for the full day of May 24th. Approximately forty-five miles to the south of Anclote Key we strike Egmont and Mullet keys, off the mouth of Tampa Bay and the main entrance to that great body of inland water.

"And because," says Herrera, "it appeared that there was an entrance between them and the coast for the ships, in order to take on water and firewood, they stayed there until the third of June, and careened one vessel called the *San Christoval*."

If you have ever sailed southward and entered the broad channel between Egmont and Mullet keys, the remarkable likeness to the scene in Herrera's description of Juan Ponce's landing place is evident at once. Sailing south from Anclote Key, passing Johns Pass, where Narváez landed later, Juan Ponce would have swept into the mile-wide passage between the two keys, both set well out in the gulf and offering wide shelving beaches, deep water almost to the mangrove roots, perfect protection from west and northwestern winds. Facing south and east were the key-dotted waters of Tampa Bay, including Shaw Point and Terra Ceia, De Soto's landing place twenty-six years later. To the right lay the Pinellas Peninsula, thickly populated with Indians, with several large villages. The entire bay, in fact, teemed with Indians. Tampa Bay had then probably the largest Indian population on the Florida gulf coast. It was an active center of Indian trade with points both north and south. The bay, alive with fish, and the mainland, a fine hunting ground, made this spot then and for centuries afterward a natural gathering point for the Timucans of western Florida. It offered food, strong protection and an ideal climate, cool in the summer and warm in the winter.

In this bountiful region Juan Ponce tarried for almost twenty days. Apparently the first ten days were passed without their being observed by the Indians. Tucked away against the shoreline vegetation of Egmont Key (now the site of old Fort Dade and the Tampa Bay Pilots' Association station and pier), it is not so surprising that Juan Ponce's fleet escaped immediate detection. The time was spent in cleaning and repairing the hull of the *San Christoval,* grass- and barnacle-laden and probably worm-eaten too, fixing the rigging of all the boats, securing water, either from springs or shallow wells, then as now easily obtainable. All the vessels in the fleet needed going over, and the crews were too busy to explore the mainland at Pinellas Point or farther south, where the large Indian settlements at Palma Sola or Terra Ceia were. On June 3rd, Herrera says, Indians showed up for the first time. The aborigines seem to have landed from their canoes and called to the Spaniards to land also. But the white men refused, and began to raise their anchor, which was in need of repair. The Indians, thinking that they meant to sail away, tried to seize the anchor chains. The Spanish sailed the smaller bark into the cluster of canoes, and broke them up. The bark's crew then went ashore and destroyed some old canoes, and also captured four women and took them aboard. The next day the Indians came back in a more friendly mood. They traded food, skins and low-grade gold, which some of the natives wore as ornaments, with the Spanish. "An Indian who understood the Spaniards, one from Hispaniola maybe," told them that they should wait, as the chief wished to trade and had gold.

This is one of the extraordinary events of the Juan Ponce exploration. Columbus had discovered the Indies only twenty-one years before. Except for the possible Amerigo Vespucci cruise of 1498, no known Spaniard or other white men had ever visited Florida. Havana had not yet been founded. Santiago, far on the eastern tip of Cuba, was the nearest Spanish colony of any importance. Hispaniola (Haiti) and San Juan (Porto Rico) were the important Spanish colonies of the time. On a direct line these were well over a thousand miles away, to be reached only by a long and dangerous ocean trip and the crossing of the entire Florida Peninsula. Yet, out from among the shouting, bickering, chattering Indians comes a voice, Indian indeed, but speaking understandable Spanish. Nothing so sharply illuminates the wide extent of inter-Indian communication in the pre-Columbian and Columbian era than this dramatic evidence that the natives of the Caribbean area kept in contact with each other. It explains, too, the immediate antagonism of the Florida Indians toward the Spanish. In the first twelve years after the discovery of Haiti and Porto Rico by Columbus it is estimated that the Spaniards killed, by fighting and enslavement, almost one million Indians from those two islands. Without question many endeavored to escape the hell the Spaniards had created in their colonies and gained the Florida coast. They must have told their story to the Tegestas and Caloosas of the south and the Timucans of the north and preached the doctrine of no intercourse and no communication. In this propaganda they were, on the whole, successful. Despite repeated effort extending over almost two centuries, the Spanish, except at St. Augustine and Pensacola, made no successful settlements, and neither St. Augustine nor Pensacola was ever safely established until the danger of Indian attack had been largely removed by the decline of these two important tribes. Though conquered and largely exterminated by the ferocious Seminole in the middle of the eighteenth century, these tribes preserved an unyielding animosity to all whites, and not until the final Seminole outbreak of 1856 did the danger of Indian attack upon white settlements in Florida forever disappear. The embittered battle for Indian peace and security against the white invaders lasted for almost three hundred fifty years.

The Haitian Indian who spoke Spanish lied to Juan Ponce. Instead of their chief's desiring trade, twenty war canoes put forth. They dashed at the anchor cables and tried to raise the anchor, with the idea of towing the Spanish ships against the near-by shallows where they could ground and then destroy them. This sounds like Haitian Indian strategy. Unable to lift the heavy anchors, they tried, but in vain, to cut the cables. Again the smaller Spanish bark raised sail and bore in heavily

among the light canoes, smashing them, killing some of
the Indians and capturing four others. The Indians
adopted other tactics, lashing two canoes together for
greater stability and striking strength. But their attack
failed against the crossbows of the Spanish and the
weight and speed of their heavier bark.

One Spaniard was lost. Either off one of the keys of
Charlotte Harbor, or the low-lying shores of Egmont Key
in Tampa Bay, the first white man was killed in battle
within the boundaries of the present United States. His
name is unknown nor is his name important. Many
more were to share his fate. On the day after the en-
counter the bark was sent to survey and sound another
harbor, in all probability south and east toward Shaw
Point on Palma Sola, or possibly off Terra Ceia where
there was a large Indian town. Despite the two skirmishes that had already taken place, Juan Ponce, a
tried Indian campaigner of the Porto Rico and Haitian
campaigns, had no respect for Indian warfare, and he
was keen to find more gold among the tribes thickly pop-
ulating the coast. The water was deep enough to float
Juan Ponce's caravels off Shaw Point and thereabouts
Juan Ponce remained until June 14th, another nine days,
fighting—and occasionally trading—with the Timucans.
The day after they arrived at their new anchorage, some
eighty Indians made their greatest effort. They attacked
one of the ships, and fought until nightfall. On this occasion Juan Ponce used his artillery as well as his cross-

bowmen, though at no time were the Spanish in any real danger of losing their vessels. The day was one more of those historical firsts connected with Juan Ponce—the first use of artillery on American soil.

The possession of gunpowder, muskets and artillery of course gave the Spaniards a tremendous advantage over the Indians. But the Spanish still relied upon the crossbow in close fighting. The Spanish crossbowmen were the best in the world. In the rush of bloody history since the discovery of the value of gunpowder in warfare, the effectiveness of medieval weapons has been underestimated. The killing range of a good crossbow was about two hundred fifty yards and its extreme range about four hundred. This compared very well with the effectiveness of the wheel-lock muskets of the period. Spanish crossbowmen were expected to hit a four-inch target at two hundred fifty yards. The crossbow sights were elevated to compensate for the drop over four hundred yards, and were fixed to permit point-blank shooting at seventy yards. The Indians had nothing but their bows and arrows to kill with, and there is no question but that the Spanish crossbowmen, without any aid from the falconets or the musketry, easily drove off any attack of Florida Indians unless they were surprised. Twenty-eight years later, De Soto fought several desperate battles with large bodies of Indians and on one or two occasions was near defeat. This, as with Cortez in Mexico, never occurred unless the Indians were in such overwhelming numbers that the Spanish simply could not kill them fast enough to hold them back from direct hand-to-hand fighting.

Yet it is a mistake to regard the Indian bow and arrow as a weapon of slight possibilities against the early Spanish soldier. The stories of the accuracy and range of effective fire of some of the North Florida Indians told by Cabeza de Vaca would be incredible if not corroborated ten years later by De Soto's soldiers who related many incidents illustrating the terrific power of penetration of the Indian's arrow within a range of two hundred yards.

"I myself," relates Cabeza in 1528, "have seen an arrow buried in a poplar stump a good half a foot." Their bows "were as thick as an arm, eleven to twelve hand spans in length," and they shot at two hundred paces with "so much sureness they miss nothing." De Soto's veterans told of a test in which two coats of mail were superimposed on each other and placed over a basket. At "one hundred and fifty paces" the arrow penetrated both at a man-killing force.

The Timucans, whose size and height amazed the Spaniards, were enemies of real worth. It was the Indian lack of ability to organize for mass attack and fear of the Spanish cavalry and dogs that were the Spanish soldiers' greatest allies.

Ponce was the first Spaniard in the New World to introduce the dog into warfare. The Spanish had used their great fighting dogs in their battles with the Moors and it was not surprising that Juan Ponce, an old veteran, should use them in his campaigns against the Indians in Porto Rico. Many Spaniards there felt the Indians were more afraid of the dogs than of the horses. Ponce brought his fighting dogs with him on his second and ill-fated trip to Florida, and both Narváez and De Soto used dogs. Several of De Soto's gained great reputations during his campaigns. Later on when dogs were used by the Spanish in their campaigns around Panama, one especially famous fighting dog was granted a captain's rank and was given a captain's pay.

The Indians had allies too, the heat, the red bugs, the mosquitoes and the gnats. Perspiring under their heavy coats of leather and steel armor, open to the insidious attack of thousands of biting, stinging, burning insects, the Spanish soldiers flung themselves into the bayous and streams in a half-crazed effort for relief, there to rouse more clouds of fierce tormentors. It was an unending battle that wore the Conquistadores out, mentally and physically, destroyed their morale and broke their will to fight, to struggle on, and finally, even to survive.

On June 14th, 1513, the Spanish had been in the bay for nineteen days. In the three battles with the Indians one Spaniard had been killed, several captives made and gold had been found. Juan Ponce had had time to size up, if not personally to explore, the general extent of his domain. His vessels were leaky, his food short. He had been three months away from Porto Rico and the crew were anxious to return. Juan Ponce was satisfied. He raised his sails and retraced his course to Dry Tortugas, arriving in just six days. Here they restored their larder with turtles, manatee—which they called seal—pelicans and terns. Not dainty fare, but filling. The Spaniard of the early sixteenth century in the Indies enjoyed strange food and grew fat on it. Juan Ponce turned south toward Cuba, east to the Bahamas, and home.

Eight years were to pass before he returned, hoping to establish the first Florida colony, but instead to receive the wound from which he died. That wound he received not far from Palma Sola shore—for he returned to Tampa Bay again, where De Soto was later to land, in his turn.

CHAPTER 6

GIVE THE PILOTS CREDIT

TAMPA BAY sweeps east and then north and west, and breaks into two broad and stubby fingers between which a thin peninsula of land projects. Upon this narrow strip of sand and humus lies the city of Tampa. The two subsidiary bays are named Old Tampa Bay and Hillsborough Bay. Why the westerly finger is called "Old" is not known. Hillsborough was named after Lord Hillsborough, who during the period of English occupation between 1763 and 1783 became interested in the whole Tampa Bay area and held a patent on a large tract of land in that vicinity. Certainly Old Tampa Bay is no older than Hillsborough or Tampa Bay proper. On Jeffery's map of 1763 Tampa Bay is properly designated as Espiritu Santo and Old Tampa Bay is called Bahia Tampa. Later when the entire body of water was christened Tampa Bay, the residents might have started calling the lesser body "Old" Tampa Bay. All three have an equal right to a solid and proper pride in their age and story. No other body of water in North America has a longer

history of Spanish exploration than Tampa Bay. By accident or by pilots' design it became the center of restless
Conquistadores seeking gold and slaves to replenish exhausted treasuries and labor pens in Cuba and Hispaniola. No other water in all North America, in that first
half century after the unveiling of the continent, was
more often the scene of fleets of bobbing caravels, of the
flash of arrow upon Spanish steel, of the hoarse battle
cries of the Estramadura against the shrill whoops of en-
raged Timucans, of desperate forays for gold and pearls,
and always, over all the smoke and fury, lay the lure of
high adventure.

None of this was wholly chance. Juan Ponce in 1513
made the Dry Tortugas the turning point for his northward cruise. His pilots brought back the word and later
explorers followed his course. Wind, current and the
general contour of the peninsula seemed to conspire to
bring the early navigators almost directly to the mouth
of Tampa Bay. Tampa Bay offered a wide and welcoming entrance, and in most places deep channels,
with attractive harbors well protected against the whip
of the northwest and southwest winds, the special curse
of gulf coast navigators, and contained withal wide
reaches inside the protecting keys in which the comparatively shallow-draft caravels could maneuver against
both wind and foe.

The pilots of the time, largely unregarded by scholars
and history, were frequently far greater factors in the

success of the early Spanish expeditions than the highly placed ones who today receive the credit. Anton de Alaminos, native of Palos, Diego Miruelo, Juan Ortubia, Juan Lopez, Alonso Pinzon were great names among the seafarers of those days. In the courts and palaces the Conquistadores strutted forward; in the glory hole, the men who manned the rudder and worked the sails knew who, above all, read the charts, sensed the seas, and rightly sniffed the weather. It was the pilots who plotted the courses and brought the vessels safely into new seas and ports. Homeward bound, Juan Ponce's fleet, threading through the Bahamas, suddenly came upon Diego Miruelo in a lone caravel. Now Don Miruelo had distinctly no business in those parts. It was Juan Ponce's exclusive territory for slave hunting or exploration. Miruelo proffered the mariner's age-old excuse that a dirty blow had propelled him unwillingly hither, and the two ships lay to, and passed the gossip of the day. De Alaminos most certainly talked with Diego Miruelo, as pilots do, despite all orders to the contrary, and he most certainly traded landfalls and channels, winds and harbors with his colleague. It is no coincidence that in 1516 Diego is found coasting up the Mangrove Coast "trading with the natives" and reporting that he has found a "beautiful bay." In the dangerous and uncertain work of traveling uncharted seas, pilots go where pilots have been. If Diego found a beautiful place to rest, the chances are that it was de Alaminos' anchorage in Tampa Bay. The year following the Cordoba expedition left Cuba on a combined exploring, gold hunting and slaving expedition. Anton de Alaminos was again "pilot major." Better than any other man in the world, de Alaminos knew that safe anchorage was to be found in Tampa Bay, where Indians were plenty and where gold had been seen and here he brought Cordoba and also Bernal Diaz, the historian, when on the fleets' way home from Mexico their ships ran out of food and water. There was gold in the Tampa Bay region. Juan Ponce traded for it on his first visit. Narváez found it in the shape of beads, tangled in a native fish net in an abandoned hut, on the day he landed just north of St. Petersburg in 1528. De Soto found the Tampa Bay Indians wearing it for decoration, and beheld a large carved wooden eagle in a native temple on Terra Ceia Island trimmed with gold. It was not common. Outside of its purely decorative qualities the Indians had no use for it, and therefore made no special efforts to secure it in their intertribal trading trips. Most of it undoubtedly came from the Georgia Indians, who found it in the hills about Dahlonega, Georgia, in small nuggets after heavy rains had fallen. The Georgian tribes traded their gold and, of more importance, their flint and other hard stone arrow heads for gulf coast sea shells, fish nets and herbs. The presence of this low grade ore excited the Spanish enormously and it was, without question, another of the impelling reasons for the frequency of their visits to the Tampa Bay region.

In the thirty-six years between 1513 and 1549, when Father Cancer made his fatal visit, there are at least nine recorded Spanish explorers who touched on or near the Tampa sector. That is an average of one exploring expedition every four years. Add to this the unreported and illegitimate hijacking slaving expeditions which certainly took place, and it is clear enough why the natives of the bay district became such fierce and unrelenting antagonists of everything Spanish.

The names read like a roll call in history. Juan Ponce, Diego Miruelo, Francisco Cordoba, Alonso Pineda, Garay, Juan Ponce again, Narváez and Cabeza de Vaca, Juan Ascano, De Soto, and Fray Cancer.

After Cancer the tide of Spanish exploration along the gulf coast ebbed away. Save for two futile visits by Pedro Menendez, Spanish interest was largely concentrated on the possibilities of east coast development. In 1565 St. Augustine was founded and the struggle between the Spanish, the French and English for the possession of northeast Florida began. Darkness descends upon the Mangrove Coast, illuminated only by brief reports of wrecks of gold-bearing galleons from Vera Cruz, smashed by treacherous currents upon Florida shoals, and of buccaneers hiding among west coast keys. The British made a few casual investigations and there were occasional reports from Cuban fishermen, who followed the kingfish and the mullet as far north as Cedar Keys, in order to reap rich harvests from the great schools that gathered in the bays that prevail along the strand. But for the most part, except for the scream of the gull and the curlew, the hoarse cough of the alligator, and the rumble of the surf along the endless miles of snow white sand, there was silence.

The explosive impact of the tremendous fact of the New World upon the Old gradually lost its novelty. The implications of the event became one of the accepted factors in the struggle for international power. After all, the expansion in geography was but one of the elements of fundamental change in the political, economic and mental lives of the people of Europe that had brought about the new day.

The twilight of the Renaissance was at hand. The world, after two hundred fifty years, was bored with the theories of the placid perfectionists who had coursed its easy paths toward the sunrise. A fresh breeze was everywhere blowing through the stuffy mentalities of Europe. New notions, new attitudes and new valuations were being established. Michael Angelo had crashed through the artistic conceptions of Florence and Flanders to create a new standard of art based on the fluidity of the mass; the conflicts of the Reformation, arising from the social pressures of the time, developed new thoughts as to the relationship of God and Man. The geography of Ptolemy gathered dust in the libraries. The time had arrived. The European mind was now ready for great adventures. And as the maps rolled back inch by inch, revealing new islands, new archipelagoes and new coast lines, "greater, my lord, than the whole coast of Spain," new ideas of place and power emerge. The days of the closet intrigue to gain the upset of a piffling principality passed. Tremendous stakes in land, in men and in metal were glittering upon the table. Never had sheer ruthlessness, complete bravery, a horse, and a sound steel sword offered such rich dividends in gold and power.

"There were ten thousand Indians assembled there," wrote Don Christopher, "but three men, well armed, and a horse or two could easily defeat them."

Men fought to gain a place aboard a caravel. The daring grasped at continents.

CHAPTER 7

DE SOTO SLEPT HERE

COMING into Bradenton today, from north or south, six miles from town the signs begin; "De Soto Trail"—with the arrow. Follow them closely. They aren't as large as they should be. The Kiwanis Club in Bradenton proposes to have some really imposing signs painted soon in the best cigar-box school of art. De Soto all armored with steel corselets and chain mail gloves will point up the Manatee and reinforce the modest roadside signs which now direct the tourist. Meantime the smaller indicators tell you what you need to know if you watch them closely and do not lose them on the quick turns. Coming north from Sarasota you turn sharply left and head directly toward the gulf coast for two miles or so and then north until you gain the banks of the broad Manatee. At this point the Manatee, easily a mile wide, is one of the most majestic stretches of water in all Florida. The land flattens out toward the river bank. An occasional mangrove marsh lies along the stream but presently the banks lift, and for a mile or two the land is occupied by a series of attractive homes whose front lawns drop softly down to the water's edge. Behind them great clumps of slash pine, interspersed with citrus groves, shoulder away the thrusts of the afternoon sun.

At the Palma Sola post office turn north again or south, it makes no difference, as both roads swing around and meet to the west. Then watch the little white signs carefully and turn once more toward the gulf coast. The end of the trail runs through a stretch of pine flats, logged-over land burnt over too in the long ago past. Little slash pine stands in the scrub. Abruptly you cross through a low hammock of bush. You are at Shaw Point, just to the southwest of the broad mouth of the Manatee, designated officially as the landing place of De Soto.

In the older books of travel, school histories written before the War Between the States, and in some of the musty yellow geographies of the 'fifties, the steel engravings of De Soto's landing picture the place as high granite cliffs with tossing surf and angry clouds. In the corners, lurking beneath the palmetto scrub, frightened and angry Indians crouch. But there are none of these things at Shaw Point. The landing place is a low shell and sand beach about ten miles from the Gulf of Mexico on the coast of Palma Sola Point in the southwestern corner of Tampa Bay. West of Tampa Bay lies the long low bulk of Anna Maria Key which shelters Palma Sola Point and the mouth of the Manatee from the occasional fury of the gales that sweep the gulf. Three keys, all famous in the early Spanish exploration of Florida and the gulf, are anchored at the entrance of Tampa Bay, Egmont, Mullet and Passage. On Egmont, the outlying key of the group, are the ruins of Fort Dade, a Spanish war fortification, now utilized by the Tampa Bay pilots and thousands of sea birds. Mullet has fortifications upon it of the same period. Passage, in De Soto's time an imposing key, has since lost all of its timber from some freak in the storms of bygone centuries. The retaining grip of the roots of the trees and undergrowth on soil has gone and the key has largely been washed away. Today it is barely visible except at low tide when hundreds of pelicans and sea gulls alight seeking crabs, small shell fish and other marine life. From the mouth of Southwest Channel, between Passage Key shoal and Egmont Key, the main southern entrance into Tampa Bay, to Shaw Point, washes a channel of an average of twelve feet. It sweeps in a long narrow path against the Point and then swings north and east across the mouth of the Manatee. Water to the west of this channel along the Palma Sola beach is very shallow, much too shallow for any large vessel to navigate. The channel offers vessels an average depth of about twelve feet which in high tide increases to seventeen. Because of this channel De Soto is believed to have selected what is now Shaw Point as the site of his landing. Accepting the general premise that De Soto did land in the Tampa Bay region and that he entered the bay through either the Passage Key or

Southwest Channel mouths, a close reading of the four journals of the expedition strongly supports this conclusion. Yet it has not been a simple matter to reach this decision. The De Soto Expedition Commission, under the chairmanship of Dr. John R. Swanton of the Smithsonian Institution, occupied four years in the study of the records of the De Soto expedition before finally finding in favor of Shaw Point. Many historians remain still unconvinced.

A short brassie shot off the shore lies Sneed's Island, which forms the north boundary of the mouth of the Manatee, and to the immediate north and east of Sneed's Island are McGill and Terra Ceia Islands. These two all but encircle a shallow, but beautiful body of water known as McGill Bay. It was on Terra Ceia Island that the principal Indian village was located. Apparently De Soto, after landing his troops, his horses and hogs and supplies, at Shaw Point made Terra Ceia Key his headquarters during the six weeks he remained in the vicinity. Shaw Point is a quiet spot. The simple granite block which the Federal government erected in May, 1939, commemorating the four hundredth anniversary of the landing of the expedition, is pleasing and inconspicuous. A considerable area has been cleared but the encroaching jungle growth makes it obvious that the Federal or State governments and the Historical Societies of Manatee and Sarasota Counties will have to take over the responsibility of maintaining the landscaping and parking of this historic spot.

The beach is compounded of heavy deposits of sea shell, mostly oyster and conch, with a litter of smaller stuff. At the water's edge clusters of mangrove and sea grape grow abundantly. This grape has special interest because the first boats returning to De Soto's fleet from the Point brought back with them "many green grapes." In the dense growth of the hammock you will find more wild grape, plenty of water oak, swamp maple and palmetto palm. When De Soto landed, May 30th, 1539, there must have been a dense growth of slash pine and live oak in the higher ground behind the beach. No point of land within the boundaries of the United States, in the first sixty years following the Columbian discovery, has greater claims to historic interest than the narrow beach at Shaw Point and the shallow reaches that prevail in front of the high mounds that now mark all that is left of the old Indian town of Terra Ceia beach on McGill Bay. There or very near there Ponce de Leon and Cordoba must have visited. Narváez's caravels, for some strange reason—it may have been a late spring fog—missed the entire mouth of Tampa Bay and sailed north for another ten miles to the much less advantageous landing at John's Pass, but Juan Anasco, De Soto's advance scout, surely visited the spot as it was he who picked it for the landing place. The massacre of Father Cancer and his devoted companions apparently took place within a stone's throw of the Point in 1549. In 1612 Lieutenant Cartayo, re-exploring Tampa Bay, Sarasota Bay and Charlotte Harbor on the orders of Governor Olivera, passed by the spot on his passage from Tampa Bay into Sarasota Bay.

De Soto had sent his comptroller, the brilliant and handsome Juan Anasco, along the Florida coast in the fall of 1538 to make a general exploration of the region and select a favorable landing place. Anasco took two caravels, and acting on the advice of Spanish skippers who knew the details of the previous voyages of the pilots de Alaminos and Miruelo, made directly for the vicinity of the bay. Anasco spent two months in and about Tampa Bay. He probably was the first European to penetrate the upper waters, at least, of Sarasota Bay, the Manatee River and Boca Ciega Bay. One story has it that Anasco was wrecked upon the keys off Tampa Bay and that while repairs were being made the entire party lived off pelicans and gulls and the fish they caught. Anasco returned to Havana with four Indians whom he had captured in the hope that they might become interpreters and guides for De Soto, and a report that gave "grand expectations of the country."

Leaving his bride Isabella de Bobadilla in Havana, De Soto sailed on May 18th, 1539. Six days later his fleet of nine vessels was slowly lifting and falling in the ground

swell off Longboat Key about eight miles north of the
New Pass entrance to Sarasota Bay.

"Having fallen four or five leagues below the port and
without any of the pilots knowing where the port lay, it
was thereupon determined that I should go in the pinnaces and look for it," wrote De Soto in his report to the
Governor at Santiago.

De Soto lowered a pinnace and taking Anasco and the
chief pilot of the expedition, Alonso Martin, and a crew
of oarsmen with him, made for the beach. De Soto probably made his first landing on North American soil on the
Longboat Key beach approximately where the Longboat
Cabana Club buildings now stand. Finding no fresh water, he took the small boat north and probably crossed to
the inside channel at the north end of Longboat just
south of Anna Maria and proceeded into Tampa Bay
through upper Sarasota Bay. This brought the party into
Tampa Bay very close to Palma Sola Point and at such an
angle that it is not surprising that Anasco did not immediately recognize the location.

The wind veered, darkness came on swiftly, and De
Soto, finding it impossible to return to his fleet, which by
this time had slowly worked up to the end of Anna Maria
Key, went ashore near Palma Sola Point where he had
observed some Indian huts. They found the huts deserted, and the fire cold. This was not surprising. The
Timucan Indians had had long and painful experience

with the Spaniards. There is no question but that among
the frequent exploring expeditions which cruised the
Mangrove Coast during the period, there were a number
of illegitimate slaving raiders from Cuba looking for opportunities to kidnap large numbers of Indians for work
on the Cuban plantations. It was these savage raids upon
the Indian camps that chiefly accounted for the almost
unexampled ferocity with which both the Timucans and
the Caloosas, who lived just to the south and centered
about Charlotte Harbor, repelled every effort on the part
of the official Spanish expeditions to develop any kind of
a working understanding.

Immediately upon their arrival off the Longboat Key
shore, De Soto's men had noted the rising columns of
signal smoke from countless Indian fires. Indian fishing
canoes had evidently spotted the Spanish fleet almost as
quickly as they hove in sight and immediately passed the
word both north and south. There were smoke signals all
about Tampa Bay. They traveled south from key to key
to Charlotte Harbor. To the north the signals crossed the
Pinellas Peninsula to warn the tribal encampments located there.

De Soto's party remained at Palma Sola overnight. In
the morning they found the fleet well off the Anna Maria
shore, some ten miles away. The men on the fleet were
worried at the absence of their leader but the offshore
wind prevented them from reaching him. Meantime De
Soto sailed his pinnace into the southwest channel and

Anasco, getting for the first time a general view of the
bay, at once recognized the Shaw Point channel entrance. Meantime a caravel had reached the pinnace and
took the party aboard. Placing a vessel on each side of
the channel to indicate the route, De Soto slowly led the
fleet toward the point. The caravels were heavily loaded,
those with the horses particularly, which, besides the animals and their feed, carried a large amount of water. It
took four days for the vessels to make a cautious approach, constantly using the lead, sounding continually
from small boats. By May 30th the bulk of the fleet was
off the Point, although two had scraped bottom on the
mud flats in getting there. Twelve days had passed since
the horses and hogs had been embarked in Cuba. It was
imperative to get the animals ashore. De Soto's plan had
been to bring the fleet up into McGill Bay, but soundings
soon proved this hopeless. Shaw Point offered the only
safe landing. Horses and hogs were disembarked and
likewise all the soldiers, only the sailors and ships' officers remaining behind. Lightened, the ships, taking advantage of the tide, turned to the northeast and edged
their way toward the Indian encampment of Ucita on
Terra Ceia Island. Next day De Soto with a hundred men
in pinnaces arrived at Ucita and took possession. Ucita
camp, like all the others, was utterly deserted. Facing the
bay was a high shell mound. Even today it is fully one
hundred yards long. At one end the mound was much
higher and upon that mound was the chief's residence.

There were several large palmetto log buildings, designed to care for several hundred persons. On the "other side of the town" was another high mound and "on top of it was a temple and on top of it, a wooden bird, with its eyes gilded. Some pearls, spoiled by fire, and of little value, were found there."

De Soto and his principal executives took over the chief's house on the high mound, and other houses were utilized for stores. The temple with its carved wooden eagle was torn down, and out of the timbers new huts constructed for the men, several men in each hut forming a mess. The low ground on the very edge of the great shell embankments was covered with dense jungle growth. De Soto ordered this cleared, to provide pasture for the horses as well as to prevent an Indian surprise. Then they posted sentinels and went to sleep.

The next day the main body of men arrived after a difficult overland march from Shaw Point. Dumped on shore at the Point Luis Moscoso, De Soto's master of the camp, had organized his men. After a scouting expedition he led the troops east along the shores of the Manatee, over the present site of Bradenton and Manatee and beyond the ruins of Braden Castle to a spot where he believed a crossing feasible. Here, with the help of small boats from the fleet, the army of six hundred and thirty men, two hundred and fifty horses and over three hundred hogs got over the stream safely and then turning sharply to the west and north, crossed the existing Tami-

ami trail where the little tomato-shipping town of Rubonia now is, and then, following close to the existing
bay-front road on Terra Ceia, worked their way through
the jungle and swamp to the shell mound Indian city of
Ucita, on the shores of McGill Bay. It must have been a
wonderful march and despite terrific difficulties per-
formed in exceedingly fast time. It was completed in less
than forty-eight hours. Much of the trip must have been
accomplished over existing Indian trails but the problem
of the transport of the horses and hogs and the handling
of the big bulk of supplies would make many a modern
soldier ponder.

At Ucita, the capital of the Timucan chief Hirrihigua's
little domain, the expedition rested for almost six weeks,
brought its supplies in from the fleet, still lying some
distance off the shore, made minor exploring expeditions
and, to the best of its ability, attempted to secure a com-
prehensible picture of the terrain and the population in
front of them. Hirrihigua's men never came back to their
village while the Spanish were there, although several
skirmishes occurred between detachments of De Soto's
men and scouting Timucans.

On the night of May 25th, 1539, when De Soto's fleet
had first been sighted by the Timucans off Longboat Key,
Juan Ortiz slept in a circle of Timucan warriors in the
tribal village of Chief Mococo. Excepting the members
of the De Soto expedition, Juan Ortiz was probably the

only white man within the whole territory of what is now the United States. Mococo was the head of a Timucan sub-tribe whose scene of operations apparently extended from the Manatee to the Alafia River and the Mococo village we think lay just north of the Alafia, close to what is now Riverview and the outer fringe of the suburbs of Tampa. Some people are magnets for romance and danger, and the life of Juan Ortiz fairly dripped with it. Born in Seville, he had as a youth managed to reach the New World, and enlisted as a member of a relief expedition sent to Florida by the wife of Panfilo de Narváez to find some trace of that tempestuous, one-eyed commander. Near what is now Clearwater Beach, Juan was lured ashore by the Indians who from the edge of the brush had waved what appeared to be a letter. Thinking that it might be news of Narváez the youngster had plunged into the water and splashed ashore. He was promptly seized and carried back to an Indian encampment occupied by Hirrihigua in the neighborhood of Safety Harbor. Ortiz was ordered burned alive, but when the flames were already singeing his shrinking body, Hirrihigua's daughter dashed in upon the scene and, as the story comes from Ortiz, pulled him from the fire and pleaded with her father for his life. All this was happening half a century before Pocahontas and John Smith were born. There was a great debate over the issue. Many of the braves and all of the medicine men were strong for the fire but in the end the chief's affection for his daughter won, and Ortiz, who had been badly burned before the rescue, was permitted to go in the company of the Indian girl who nursed him back to strength. The anti-Ortiz faction, however, continued to demand his death. To let him live, they said, would ruin both the fishing and the corn crop. The medicine men in the village were pressing. Ortiz was on the eve of being sentenced again when the Indian woman made and won a second plea.

It was the custom of the Timucans to place their dead, immediately after death, in the branches of trees, in a distant and obscure spot, and there permit the corpse to rot. After a year the bones were buried with considerable ceremony. It was regarded as vital that the body be undisturbed during this time. The business of guarding the spot, reeking with odors and alive with the prowling wild cats, puma, wolves and lesser animals, was a most unpleasant and dangerous one. It was often given to convicted Indian criminals, who could accept it in lieu of death. Such a job being at the moment open, Ortiz's defender proposed him to the chief. Ortiz took it. His duty was to guard the cemetery grove all night. Still weak, he became violently ill the first night. In the midst of a spasm he saw a wild cat attempting to carry off the body of a child. With scarcely enough strength to bend his bow he loosed an arrow and, by fortune, killed the animal. Again, by fortune, some Indians, delegated to check up on the new guardian, arrived just in time to witness the event. That he had killed the animal and saved the body so raised him in the esteem of the Timucans that for nearly a year he was permitted to perform his ghastly job without harassment.

As autumn drew near the medicine men began again to clamor for Ortiz's death at the coming harvest celebration. The pressure this time was not to be resisted. One night the Indian "princess" with her attendant stole to the cemetery to warn Ortiz to leave Hirrihigua's town. He must flee at once. She told him that she was pledged to Chief Mococo and was to be married soon; that she would give the Spaniard a beaded skin that would contain a message to Mococo to insure his safety. She would see that he was guided to the Mococo village. Ortiz escaped. Being a true Spaniard, he relates how high his hopes were that the princess' interest in him was more than merely a tender heart. His hopes expressed gained him nothing but a calm rebuff. Angry, Hirrihigua tried hard to get Ortiz back, even refusing to permit his daughter's marriage with Mococo for some years. Ortiz at the Mococo camp was given some degree of freedom, but according to the story he related to De Soto, he never traveled far from the village lest he might fall into Hirrihigua's hands.

When the Indian scouts announced the arrival of a Spanish fleet off the mouth of the bay, Mococo sent Ortiz to contact them. Ortiz, with a party of nine Indians, pushed south toward the mouth of the Manatee and there fell in with a party of forty Spanish horsemen under

command of Baltasar de Gallegos. Anasco, the year before, had heard a vague rumor of a Spanish prisoner
among the Tampa Bay Indians and De Soto had sent
Gallegos out to find him. When the Spaniards sighted the
Indians they attacked the party furiously. Ortiz leaped
forward, holding up his arm and shouting. But dressed
in Indian clothing as he was and browned as dark as any
Timucan, a Spanish horseman dashed at him with his
sword raised high. Ortiz attempted to cry out in Spanish.
To his horror he suddenly discovered he could remember no Spanish words. In choking desperation he
gasped "Seville—Seville—Christian—Christian." Saved, he
brought his party to De Soto and told his story. From that
time forward he became a most valuable member of De
Soto's staff. As an interpreter and guide he was invaluable. He cemented the Mococo-De Soto friendship; ar-
ranged the visit by De Soto to Mococo's town, and later,
when De Soto left Terra Ceia for the vicinity of Ocala,
himself visited Mococo again. Ortiz remained with the
De Soto expedition until the early winter of 1542. He
died on the banks of the Arkansas River where De Soto
was encamped.

In the matter of extensive preparation and the assem-
bly of supplies for his expedition, De Soto was the Admiral Byrd of his time. He brought with him great
quantities of munitions, steel corselets, wheel-locks, crossbows, arrows, tanned hides, nails, tools, even lum-

ber. Planning a possible colony somewhere along the Florida beach, he also brought with him bundles of seeds and grain. Yet, curiously, nothing seems to have survived the expedition. La Salle, when he went down the Mississippi, mentions finding a Spanish sword and a piece of armor in an Indian tent on the lower river which he surmises probably came from De Soto's stores. The present site of the Hirrihigua town mounds belongs to Mr. E. C. Abel, of Manatee County. In the extensive deposits he has found many shells obviously ground and reshaped for human use, drilled for ornaments and utilized as light club heads or even hoes. There are piles of shards of pottery but he has found only one thing that might relate to the De Soto occupation. Some years ago working on the site of the old shell mound where Hirrihigua's cabin stood, the one De Soto used the first night after his landing, Mr. Abel did find an old Spanish medal with a religious image on it. Unfortunately, before the medal was examined by an archeologist, the little decoration became misplaced. With it perhaps was lost a possible connecting link between the visit of De Soto's troops and the present day. De Soto died in the summer of 1542 on the banks of the Mississippi south of Memphis and was buried in the great river close to the west bank "in a coffin of elm bark." The secret river burial in the night was decided upon in order to avoid confessing his death to the Indians so soon. When he died the records of the expedition note that there were still two hundred horses in the party and that the hogs had increased from three hundred fifty on their arrival to upward of seven hundred head. These animals were the personal property of De Soto, and upon his death, they were auctioned off to the soldiers. Most of the horses died in the following year and a half before the arrival of the remnant of the expedition in Mexico, but legend holds to it that the half-wild razor-back hogs found in northwest Florida and southern Georgia are from the original De Soto herd. The Indians became passionately fond of hog meat and took great risks to raid the pens erected by the expedition. De Soto frequently gave pairs of them away as gifts to chiefs and, on one occasion when the expedition back-tracked, they found an Indian's pair had raised a litter.

Swing off the Tamiami trail to the left at Rubonia, about ten miles north of Bradenton, along the delightful coast road, and you come upon the great temple mound with unexpected suddenness. The main road runs to the right of it and a local "dirt" road to the left leaving the mound in the center of a long and narrow triangle. The mound itself is fully forty feet high but so thickly have the live oaks grown, as well as a clump of graceful cabbage palm, that the average automobile traveler might pass it without a second glance.

"Yes, the mound is there all right," said a passing farmer of whom I asked directions. "You look sharp and you will see it. Better take the right hand road and stop at the little house on the side of the road. The house is deserted now but a path to the top of the mound runs from the main road just back of it. And say," he remarked as he waved good-by, "I don't want to scare you, but keep your eyes peeled—there are rattlers around in that brush."

The little gray house was easy to find. Behind it the path to the mound runs twenty-five yards through light underbrush and cabbage palm. Then the ramp to the mound sweeps upward abruptly. The great pile of shell and muck faces the east, and the ramp rising to the crest comes up from the west. For two hundred yards toward the shell mounds on McGill Bay beach at the Abel farm is a low cleared space. In this ground people say skulls have often been found. It may have been a community burying ground. The Timucans, however, generally buried their dead in mounds, sometimes several skeletons to a mound, never so many as this burying ground seems to suggest. Mr. Abel inclines to the belief that at some date before the Spanish occupation an epidemic swept the village. So many may have died that the Indians could not follow their customary ceremonials and may have had to bury their dead in one common trench.

Smaller than the vast ceremonial pyramids of Central America, the mound has many of the same characteristics. The way it faces the east shows that the Timucans, like the Mayans of Yucatan, worshiped the sun. The western ramp is similar to the Central American Indian construction practice. This is no place for detailed discussion of the degree of relationship or contact which may have existed between the Mayans of Yucatan and Guatemala and the Timucans of the Mangrove Coast. But on evidence unearthed in recently discovered Florida mounds, and from the many proofs of wide travel between the Indians of the Central American area and the West Indies, it is impossible not to be strongly impressed with the belief of Timucan-Mayan contact. The distances between Florida, Cuba and Yucatan are much too short—there are too many evidences of Mayan-Timucan commerce found in the numerous burial mounds located on the keys and along the banks of the Manatee.

It is clear that the active life of the village was conducted on the McGill Bay side. At one time local people said a smaller mound stood a short distance from the large temple mound but treasure hunters have completely demolished it. Such treasure hunters have dug a large hole into the west slope of the big mound. Nothing has ever been found and there is no reason to believe that anything will be. The mound was purely ceremonial and not a burial mound. Only in the burial mounds are pottery, artifacts, etc. found. Local residents tell how one time a treasure hunter "from the north" visited the temple site with a "gold detector." After a good deal of marching back and forth—at night in the moonlight—he declared that gold would be found in the mound's center.

The big hole remains where he and his companions dug. They found nothing.

The temple mound and the shell mounds on the Abel farm are historically significant. Not only were they the political and religious center of a large tribe of the Timucan Indians under Chief Hirrihigua, whose bitter hatred of all Spaniards dated apparently from the Narváez expedition of 1528 when his mother, it is believed, was assaulted and badly injured by dissolute Spanish soldiers, but it marks for us one of the most certain resting spots of Hernando De Soto on the North American continent. De Soto led his North American expedition for three years from the date of his landing until his death on the banks of the Mississippi. He traversed much of northwestern Florida, southeastern and central Georgia, southwestern South Carolina, the tip of southwestern North Carolina, southeastern Tennessee, almost all of Alabama and northern Mississippi. Yet in all that long trek there are few precise places where one can state with any positiveness, "on this spot De Soto slept." I know of but two. One, the gray and grim old fortress of La Fuerza of Havana, the oldest fortification in that city, which De Soto himself largely constructed. There he left the ripely beautiful Isabella de Bobadilla to await his return. The other is the shell mounds of Terra Ceia Bay.

The main body of De Soto's fleet returned to Havana

and the lonely Isabella de Bobadilla as soon as they were free of their cargo. Several vessels, however, were retained and on July 9th De Soto sent his famous letter to the Governor of Santiago on the progress of the expedition by Vasco Porcallo, who had been the original choice as De Soto's chief assistant. Porcallo, a large land and mine owner in Cuba, quickly developed a great distaste for Florida. His main interest anyway may have been to find slaves to work his Cuban mines. After a brush or two with Hirrihigua's Timucans, he must have seen that the Florida Indian was a proposition very different from the smaller and timid Carib. After a week's halt De Soto, with the main body of his soldiers and Indian carriers, started northeast to catch up with Gallegos, who had gone ahead to investigate reports of a large Indian community near what is now Ocala, where gold and food might be found. At Terra Ceia he left Peter Calderon with some forty horsemen, sixty foot soldiers, camp followers and the sailors from the single caravel still remaining. They were to hold the point until further orders. These troops seem to have kept close to McGill Bay. In October Calderon received his orders. He was to break camp, leave what stores he could not easily take with him to Chief Mococo, and rejoin De Soto. Mococo received from Calderon, according to the Garcilaso narrative, over five hundred quintals of cassava, many cloaks, coats and pairs of footwear along with a large amount of shields, cuirasses, pikes, lances and helmets. Some day perhaps mounds along the Alafia or the headwaters of the Little Manatee may be uncovered and give up bits of some of this steel armament. Such a royal gift in munitions must have enormously increased Mococo's prestige among the Timucan sub-tribes. The caravel returned to Havana with messages to the waiting Isabella, who, they say, paced the wide stone ramparts of Fuerza, or sewed in the little pink stone tower which then, and now, decorates its southwest corner. In the depths of the crude old structure, behind its glassless windows, set deep with double iron grilles, in the eighteen-foot walls were her apartments which can still be seen. But on the fort's wide ramparts the bright sun of Havana poured over her. She could look east across the narrow waters of the harbor to the gleaming sides of Casa Blanca hill, where the Observatory now stands, or down the harbor, over the site where Morro Castle was later built, across the low fortifications of La Punta, just then being raised. She could gaze across the indigo blue of the Caribbean waters toward Florida, where her straining eyes had last seen the slowly dipping sails of De Soto's fleet disappear in the swift twilight of the tropic evening. Isabella waited with Leonora, eighteen-year-old wife of the dashing Nuno de Tobar, whose impetuous suit for the hand of Leonora almost won him a duel with De Soto, Leonora's guardian, before her marriage on the eve of the fleet's departure.

The two waited as did so many Spanish wives. They

prayed. And then one day there was no longer any reason at all for Isabella to wait. Still she lingered, some say, to die in Havana. Others say that after a time she gathered her strength and resolution and, taking Leonora, she returned once more to Seville.

It was Pedro Menendez de Aviles, who hanged his French captives from Fort Caroline not because they were French but because of his distaste for their Protestantism, who first brought Jesuit missionaries to Florida in 1567. Two of these, Brothers Villareal and Rogel, were established in a small mission, guarded by a contingent of soldiers, on Biscayne Bay near the present city of Miami. Later Brother Rogel went on to the Mangrove Coast, establishing missions at Charlotte Harbor and Tampa Bay. The missions were small and flimsy affairs and the Indians' reaction to the spiritual teachings of the Jesuits was not enthusiastic. "Rogel had some corn," reported a brother Jesuit later, "which attracted the Indians to him to the extent that they heard the doctrine, but when the maize was exhausted their attendance ceased."

The meager records show that the two good brothers endured starvation, suffered the tortures of insect attack and the ills of the body. Little was accomplished in a spiritual way and the missions at Tampa Bay and Charlotte Harbor were abolished, but it was at the Biscayne Bay mission, so far as we know, that the first dramatic performance of a secular nature was staged within that part of the new world which is now the United States. Florida history is a mine of unexpected dates.

Life on Biscayne Bay in the summer of 1568 was not only hard but desperately dull. Busy about his mission tasks, bargaining for holdover corn from shrinking Indian stores, fighting mosquitoes, red bugs and the "misery," Brother Villareal sensed the deadly boredom of the soldiers. Something must be done. He had tried "fiestas with litanies to the Cross," but for St. John's Day when the Governor was expected, he put on his real surprise.

Brother Villareal produced two "comedies." "The plays," wrote Brother Villareal to Rogel, "had to do with the war between men and the world, the flesh and the devil." The soldiers, he added, enjoyed the plays very much. We can well believe it. His formula was good three hundred and seventy-five years ago on the shores of Biscayne Bay. It is still sound dramatic provender both in Hollywood and Broadway in 1942.

Then for half a century the Mangrove Coast lay forgotten. The grim struggle between the cold-eyed Catherine de Medici in Paris and the even clammier-hearted Philip in Madrid absorbed all the thoughts and energies of the servants of both crowns. There was no gold on the Mangrove Coast, and the Indians being tough and savage, the Very Magnificent in Madrid decreed that all traffic on the gulf coast be abandoned. The Spanish crown concentrated on gaining a permanent foothold on the East Coast and to seeing to it that the lilies of the Bourbons never blotted the bright blue of the Florida skies.

For half a century only the doddering clerks in the archives of the Indies in Seville ever glanced at the west Florida charts—those charts on which old red-haired Panfilo de Narváez and the beautifully dressed De Soto had with eager eye and high hope traced out their rendezvous with death. Then there came a day when the European tension eased. Almost fifty years had passed since the first palmetto huts had been thrown up at St. Augustine; almost a hundred since Juan Ponce de Leon had tried to establish the first Spanish colony in Florida along the gulf coast. People had time again for interest and curiosity about Virginia and the "coast of Apalache and the Bay of Carlos."

Juan Fernandez de Olivera, governor of all the Floridas, in his palm-thatched mansion in St. Augustine also had time to spare and had been looking around. He dispatched Lieutenant Juan Rodriguez de Cartayo in the summer of 1612 with a party of twenty soldiers and a pilot, to the Tampa Bay region, to report fully on the situation especially as to the attitude of the Indians. Reaching the Bay of Pooy, as Tampa Bay was then known to the Spanish, Cartayo held a "friendly meeting with the Indians." Securing canoes the party moved

across the bay and entered the "Rio de Tampa," now
known as Sarasota Bay. Working south through Sarasota
Bay, where he was frequently halted at the Indian villages to receive presents of fish and fruit, he took the
outside route south of the existing city of Venice and
entered Charlotte Harbor. Sixty canoes, wrote Cartayo
in his report to the governor, welcomed him when his
party arrived at Charlotte Harbor. Carlos, the chief of
the Caloosas, after some diplomatic hesitation, agreed
to meet Cartayo in the middle of the bay. Here Carlos
arrived in a great canoe manned by more than forty
Indians. The Indian chief presented Cartayo with two
plaques of gold, each weighing about two ounces, such
as the Indians were accustomed to wear on their fore-
heads on ceremonial occasions. He also gave the Spaniard a Negro slave who had been deposited upon their
shores from the wreck of some Spanish vessel en route
presumably to Mexico.

Governor Olivera wrote to His Majesty how Cartayo
had reported on the beauties of the great Bay of Pooy
which "is where the Adelantado Hernando De Soto
landed and owing to its extent there can enter a fleet of
fleets." The governor urged the immediate construction
of a fort on the bay as a center for a gulf coast colony
and a protection against pirates. Nothing happened. By
the time Olivera's report reached the gloomy Escorial
more important matters had intervened. Florida was far
away. The King was bored with colonies.

CHAPTER 8

TARDY LAURELS: BARON KREBS
AND HIS COTTON GIN

IT sometimes takes a century or two to down a legend, or rewrite a bit of history so that a slightly different light is cast on some of the better known dates in history. The northern school books and the southern ones too all pay tribute to Eli Whitney as the inventor of the cotton gin. All the same, the first successful commercially operated cotton gin was put in operation on the gulf coast at Pascagoula, Mississippi, twenty years before Whitney completed his first model. He first filed his application for a patent upon a cotton gin June 20th, 1793, and received the patent on March 14th, 1794.

Yet in the summer of 1771, twenty-two years before, Baron Hugh Ernestus Krebs fixed up and placed in operation on his big plantation near Pascagoula in the French colony of Louisiana, as it was then, a treadle-operated roller-type gin that could clean upward of 80 pounds of cotton a day. That was double what slave labor could do. Krebs, in his workshop, kept at it. His next gin stepped the output up. His gin could do four times the work of a slave. One slave-driven power wheel could work a series of gins hooked together and run in series.

"The Concise Natural History of East and West Florida" by one Bernard Roman, published in 1775, tells the story. The cosmographer of the Florida coast visited Baron Krebs at his plantation in 1772, when he was making his tour of the coast between the Mississippi delta and Cedar Keys, and was greatly interested by what he found happening in the Baron's workshop.

Cotton had been planted on the Louisiana gulf coast for over fifty years when Roman visited Krebs and saw the first gin in operation. Charlevoix saw cotton growing in Natchez as early as 1721 and there had been a slowly increasing demand for the thread, despite the difficulties of cleaning the bloom of the entangling seed. Cotton acreage in the far south rose slowly but steadily. The problem of relieving the bloom of the sticky seed early engaged the attention of the planters. Dupratz constructed one machine to remove the seed but the apparatus failed to work. Probably Baron Krebs had heard of the Dupratz experiment and had gone to work to develop a model of his own. Or, just as likely, Krebs may have taken over some local model, constructed by some unknown and unrecorded plantation genius, and developed it.

Roman's interest in the Krebs gin was keen on sight. In fact, Roman's enthusiasm was so hot that the worthy

Baron became a little disturbed and even annoyed. In the end he would not let Roman examine his latest improved model.

The Krebs gin, wrote Roman in 1772, "is a strong frame of four studs, each about four feet high and joined above and below by strong traverse pieces. Across these pieces are placed two round, well polished iron spindles, having a small groove through their whole length, and by means of treddles are by the workman's foot put in directly opposite motions to each other; the workman sits before the frame having a thin board of seven or eight inches wide and the length of the frame before him; this board is so fixed to the frame that it may be moved, over again, and near the spindles; he has the cotton in a basket near him and with his left hand spreads it on this board along the spindles which, by their turning, draw the cotton through them, being wide enough to admit the cotton but too near to permit the seed to go through, which being thus forced to leave the cotton in which it was contained, and by its rough coat entangled; falls on the ground between the workman's legs while the cotton drawn through falls on the other side into an open bag suspended for the purpose under the spindles. The French in Florida have much improved this machine by a large wheel, which turns two or three mills at once, and with so much velocity as by means of a boy, who turns it, to employ two negroes at hard labor to shovel the seed away from under the mill: one of these machines I saw at Mr. Krebs at Pasagoocoola but it was partly taken down, he claiming the invention, was very cautious in answering my questions, I cannot describe it accurately; I am informed that one of these improving mills will produce seventy to eighty pounds of clean cotton per diem."

Eighteenth-century punctuation and sentence structure dims the clarity of the description of the machine. But there seems to be no question as to the fact that the machine was successfully operated.

What records we have seem to show that Baron Hugo Ernestus Krebs was Alsatian born in Neumagen on the Moselle. There were several German settlements along the upper gulf coast, both in French Louisiana and near-by Spanish Pensacola and it is presumed that Baron Krebs arrived in America some time about the middle of the eighteenth century. He took up a large tract of land on the lower Pascagoula river, near Pascagoula, Mississippi. A man of considerable means, he purchased many Negroes, constructed a manorial home and planted cotton, indigo and rice. He is said to have also owned the schooners which transported his produce to the wharfs at New Orleans. He died about 1776 leaving fourteen children whose descendants still owned portions of the old Krebs plantation within the last decade.

Thomas Arkwright did not put his roller spinner into operation until 1769. The roller spinner greatly increased the production of cotton thread but it was not until 1773 when Strutt invented the weaver that cotton really came into its own. British industrialists moved slowly. The Arkwright spinner and the Strutt weaver did not revolutionize the industry overnight. But by the end of twenty years the improved methods of cotton production had begun to create real demand upon the planters for more and more cotton. The mills in the Lancashire country cried for it and the nimble fingers of the slave women and children in the cleaning barns of the plantations of the South could not keep up with the demand.

The times were ripe for something to relieve the pressure. Young Eli Whitney, traveling in Georgia, arrived at the Phineas Miller plantation at Mulberry Grove. Within ten days he had a model gin in operation. Within a year he was building gins, and with his patent from the new United States Patent Office in his possession he was unable to build gins fast enough. The Whitney gin, in perfect mechanical harmony, was the crest of the wave thrown up by the inventions of Arkwright and Strutt. The days of King Cotton had begun.

There seems to have been a basic similarity between the Whitney and Krebs gins. Both were obviously working along the same lines, with the same tools and materials. But apparently neither Baron Krebs nor his heirs made any effort to extend the use of his invention. There was no compelling need in 1772. Hand-cleaned cotton filled amply the needs of British and European manufacturers. It is even doubtful if Eli Whitney had ever heard of the Krebs machine. There was plenty of litigation with the Whitney patents later on, and it is likely that if the Krebs invention had been widely known, the fact of the prior invention of the Krebs gin would have been seized upon by some litigant as a factor in these suits.

We can say now merely, "Krebs was ahead of his time." Eli Whitney makes the history books as much for "perfect timing" as for invention. Krebs' laurels are there, however, for those who enjoy the discovery of facts in out-of-print books.

CHAPTER 9

PIRATE, PADRE OR PRESS AGENT

ON July 19th, 1900, Johnny Gomez was drowned fishing for mullet off Panther Key. Death strikes often at the men who spend their lives following the schools of mullet and king as they roam northward along the squall-tossed beaches of the Gulf of Mexico. One death more or less excites little comment. But Johnny Gomez was different. Johnny was a hundred and nineteen years old, and for forty years he had been the outstanding testimonial of the salubrity of the Gulf Coast climate. Year after year, decade after decade, Johnny had lived on in his little house on Panther Key. Panther Key, with its long, white beach, is one of the outer fringe of keys dotting the northern boundary of Ten Thousand Islands. Johnny, whose story was that his real name was Juan, reached Panther Key in 1876 when he was already ninety-five years old. He brought his wife along, a matron of a little over fifty, and set up at once as a fisherman and beachcomber. His income fairly regularly refused to stretch, and the county commissioners of what was then Lee County would do the needful up to eight dollars a month. It was in the course of establishing Johnny's claim, as an aged gentleman out of funds, upon the bounty of Lee County that the vital statistics about his early life became a matter of record. He was born, so he said, in Portugal in 1781 and moved to Bordeaux with his family when he was twelve. That was the year Johnny saw Napoleon.

"He sat on a big horse and the soldiers all marched past and cheered him. I saw them," said Johnny.

He signed, the year after that, as a cabin boy on an American vessel bound for Charleston, S. C. He deserted his first day in port, and from Charleston drifted south to St. Augustine. Then he took to the sea again. All the thirty middle years of Johnny's life story remain hidden in a fog. He would run on about some terrific hurricane he was in on some voyage to Havana, or mention in passing a fight with privateers off Cape Antonio. All he could prove was that about the time the United States established Fort Brooke at Tampa, in the year 1823, he was around as a sailor on a coastwise trading boat. After that he went to mule driving along the army trail from Tampa Bay to Fort Myers and in the Seminole wars Johnny swore he served under Zachary Taylor at the battle of Lake Okeechobee, that Christmas Day of 1837. His tales of the Civil War were of blockade running. Johnny was eighty when the war started and an old man already by almost anyone's standards. Captain W. D. Collier says he saw Johnny in 1859 lift two bags of salt, each weighing two hundred pounds, and carry them on his back up a near-by hill. After the Civil War and the opportunities it offered were out of the way, Johnny bobs up next around Clearwater, where, it seems, he had a brother. The brother died in the 'seventies and Johnny moved to Panther Key.

Soon after he settled on the key, Johnny first began to talk about the mysterious gap in his early life. On one occasion, and at first only briefly, he admitted that he had once or twice been mixed up with pirates. Interested inquirers got him going. Once loquacious, he began to give details—a story or two about sudden dashes from behind low-lying keys upon some helpless becalmed merchantman, sudden attack and death and rape. Once in an outpouring of reminiscences, Johnny is reported to have said he had seen "a hundred men walk the plank." Interesting and illuminating, if true, but in all the long and dirty record of marine racketeering on the gulf, a forty-year stretch, there is no authenticated incident of anybody at all ever being compelled to go through that famous ritual. Murder there was in great and bloody plenty and a horrid lot of top-deck torture of the simpler kind—hot irons to the soles of men's bare feet, twisted arms, and half-choked victims, wildly kicking, suspended from yards—but nothing so dramatic or so swift and easy, from the victim's viewpoint, as "walking the plank."

On one high occasion when Johnny was at his best

about the days when he was the bad, old rogue, he first told the story of the Little Spanish Princess.

"In 1801," Johnny is supposed to have started off, "there was a Spanish Princess down in Mexico. She had been entertained most royally by all the first families of Spain's richest colony and before her return she offered to let travel back with her eleven daughters of Mexico's great haciendas and to see that these precious maids were properly 'finished,' and introduced to the court at Madrid. Her proposal, with its hinted promise of fine marriages in Spain, was accepted, and when a royal galleon of the yearly treasure fleet sailed away from Vera Cruz, it carried the Princess and her retinue of Mexican maidens ensconced in its cabins. Blown off its proper course, the ship was moving some forty miles off Charlotte Harbor, when a pirate craft came athwart its path. The great ship and its metal and human treasure was made captive."

Pause for breath. We must bring in Gasparilla, slightly out of sequence. We have more to say later about this Gasparilla.

The pirate in the Johnny Gomez story was this very Gasparilla, the one who haunted the keys of Charlotte Harbor to snare just such unwary vessels as the great and royal treasure galleon from Vera Cruz.

Gasparilla, now the master, spurned the products of the best haciendas of Old Mexico and tossed them brutally to his crew. For himself the Spanish Princess, and to her he put the proposition bluntly!

"She slapped him," Johnny said, "smartly." Whereupon Gasparilla drew his sword. In one clean cut he sliced the royal head off.

Sometimes in his stories that is where it ended. But one time at least Johnny went on with the story, even took a party to Little Gasparilla Key where, pointing to a grave, he told them the pirate, confounded with remorse, had buried the lady there. The mound was opened. There are those along the Mangrove Coast who swear they heard and saw that day, and that when the grave was opened a female skeleton was found—with the skull sliced off.

Now Gasparilla, the pirate, came into none of Johnny's earlier stories and the best piratical research of today sets Johnny down as his creator. That seems to be too generous to Johnny. He must have had outside help—and this one has to admit—from other fanciful men, or from facts in the long and crimson saga of the pirate Gasparilla, curse of the Mangrove Coast. Far more piratical lore than Johnny ever could have acquired in his simple unlettered life is interwoven in the career of the bloody Gasparilla. There must have been some real Gaspar at the start. Johnny, like many another free lance reporter or large-hearted rewrite man, at any rate, stood sponsor for it. Johnny, the short, thick-set fellow with dark eyes dancing and glowing despite his hundred years and with a famous fondness for the amber rum of Havana, stuck to his stories. Whenever a Cuban drink was in question, what if the gentleman doing the buying wanted pirates for his money? He was ready. As for Gasparilla, well, why not Gasparilla, as good a name as any?

As good as any? Better!

It was a name with punch; it had appeal, and it had the very sound of buccaneers in it. It pleased the officials of the old Charlotte and Northern Railroad. It was there on the maps as Gasparilla Key, Little Gasparilla Key, and Gasparilla Pass, along with Captiva Island and Sanibel Key for so many years the oldest residents of Fort Myers or Boca Grande, took it all for history. So, if there had been pirates around about the gulf and if old Johnny Gomez remembered all about one of them, what was more likely than that his name had been Gasparilla!

The railway folders of the Charlotte and Northern Railroad put it all in print, the story of Gasparilla, the pirate, and his "brother-in-law" Johnny Gomez. The printed pamphlet, as has happened in history before, became the outstanding "authority" for the legend of Gasparilla, scourge of the Gulf Coast. Bradlee, the author of "Piracy in the West Indies," a scholarly job, and Gosse, in his famous "Pirates' Who's Who," all report on Gasparilla and all name their source as the railroad advertising pamphlet. For, in fact, there is no other authori-

tative source to be found in America. Gasparilla, says
the legend, had accumulated some thirty million dollars
in loot which he cached in pits on little Gasparilla Key.
His harem of captured females he kept on Captiva Island. Sanibel was his hunting preserve. Gasparilla, it is
said, was born in Barcelona, educated for the Spanish
Navy, was captain of a Spanish frigate, "stole the crown
jewels" and with a crew of Catalonian cronies with
loose morals, sped for the wilds of the Caribbean and
the dim, blue coast of Florida. This, I quote from one of
the most "authoritative of the pirate's biographies," was
about 1783, and here on the keys that rim that beautiful
bay, he ruled and ravaged, raped and ruined for almost
forty years. Then, on a day late in 1821, when he and his
ruffianly crew were gathered together for a final dividend, a strange and seductive sail appeared. It looked
like a Liverpool merchantman, loaded low with Man-
chester and Sheffield ware, soft English sovereigns, and
perhaps, some wealthy passengers. This sight, avows
the legend, was more than the old reprobate could en-
dure and, with a shout, he led his men aboard his boat,
lying safely in the lee of Little Gasparilla Key. Out they
shot through the channel and into the Gulf to engage
the Englishman. As they did so, the British flag slipped
down, the American flag went up, the canvas disguises
fell away and lo and behold, there was the *Enterprise,*
the plucky little *Enterprise,* the United States Naval
sloop whose name had become a symbol of sudden

death to all bad-minded mariners along the Florida straits, with Lieutenant Lawrence Kearny in command. After a blast or two, old Gasparilla wrapped himself in his anchor chains and jumped overboard. Some of the crew did likewise and the rest "were hanged in New Orleans." This, it is written, was presumed to have occurred on December 21st, 1821, off Boca Grande on Charlotte Harbor.

So the thirty-million-dollar dividend was never voted, the pirates' stronghold disappeared, the fortunate rascals who escaped went far away. And only Johnny Gomez came back to tell the tale but not to locate the treasure.

"Johnny never had the price of a shirt for his back," mused another pioneer the other day. He had known the old mullet fisherman well. "But at that," he went on, "I think Johnny knew something about pirates, pirates along the Cuban coast maybe, not here."

A point to stick at in the Gasparilla story and its stirring finale is the proven fact that it could never have finished that way. On December 21st, 1821, the date on which Lieutenant Kearny was presumed to be blasting Gasparilla out of the water off Boca Grande, the Lieutenant and the little *Enterprise*, the gamest cockerel in either the Caribbean or the Gulf, was two hundred fifty miles away off Cape Antonio, the west tip of Cuba, disposing of a gang of cut-throats in a twenty-five-ton sloop he had pursued into the shallow waters of the Cuban coast. The men escaped but the Lieutenant captured the sloop and used her for a tender for a time afterward. He gave a full account of that day's work not only to Commander Daniel T. Patterson, in charge of naval operations, but also in a report direct to the Secretary of the Navy.

If Gasparilla ever was a pirate, the wickedest who ever marauded the palm-strewn shores of the Caloosahatchee, he was certainly unknown to the navy. He went unlisted by the special anti-pirate squadron sent into the Gulf in 1821. Neither his name nor the name of any man charged with being or admitting to have been a member of his crew is noted in the grim records of the Federal Courts. American State Papers have no trace of him. Spanish archives may have some record of the old gentleman who, in some wicked manner, got custody of the jewels of the Spanish crown. In Washington he is unknown.

One account tried to tie his seamy name to the story of the pirate "Richard Coeur de Lion," who captured the Philadelphia packet *Orleans* and held her for two days of good, sound plundering, then got away before approaching relief could catch him. As the pirate shoved off with sixty thousand dollars in cash and a cargo of dry goods and stores, he handed a note to the captain of the *Orleans*. It read:

"At Sea and In Good Luck.

"Sir: Between buccaneers, no ceremony; we take your dry goods and, in return, I sent you pimento; therefore we are now even; I entertain no resentment.

"Bid good-day to the officer of the United States, and tell him that I appreciate the energy with which he has spoken of me and my companions at arms. Nothing can intimidate us; we run the same fortune, and our maxim is 'that the goods of the world belong to the brave and the valiant.' The occupation of Florida is a pledge that the course I follow is conformable to the policy pursued by the United States.

Richard Coeur de Lion."

The attack on the *Orleans,* according to Commander Patterson at New Orleans, took place in mid-September off Abaco, Bahamas, many hundreds of miles from Boca Grande and the Gulf of Mexico.

Admitted there never was a pirate Gasparilla, still there must have been someone of that name because, long before such a Gasparilla was ever invented, with Charlotte Harbor as headquarters and Captiva Island the site of his harem, old Spanish and English charts of Charlotte Harbor show the name Gasparilla. In some maps it is attached to the keys, still known as Gasparilla Key and Little Gasparilla Key. Captiva and Sanibel are recorded in the same way. It is obvious that the name was an old one and noteworthy. As late as 1772, Bernard Roman, in charting the gulf coast for his great map, dedicated to the New York Marine Society, indicated Boca Gasparilla and likewise Boca Captiva and Sanybel

Island. In his journal, Roman maintained that it was he who discovered the Miakka River and the Peace River, and for years the charts had the Miakka as the Roman River. Roman did his chart work nine years at least before the piratical Senor Gasparilla is alleged to have first made his appearance. So someone long before the "pirate" placed the name on Florida's maps.

A clue to all this, but only a clue, is afforded in certain of the Spanish and American maritime reports of the middle of the last century, discovered by Dr. Mark Boyd of Tallahassee.

The "American Coast Pilot" for 1842 says, "Carlos Bay is a large entrance made in the coast, in which are emptied various rivers, whose mouths are covered by many keys and shoals, which leave between them many channels more or less wide; the northernmost is called Friar Gaspar, and has six feet of water, the next is called Boca Grande, the deepest, having fourteen feet of water."

Friar Gaspar—not Pirate Gaspar.

Again the Spanish chart book for 1862 published in Madrid; *"Derrotero de las Islas Antillas y de las Costas Orientales de America"* states even more interestingly, "The inlet of Friar Gaspar or Gasparillo. The Inlet of Friar Gaspar, which is the most northerly of those which lead to Carlos Bay, is situated to the north of the northern point of Gasparilla Key."

Friar Gaspar again.

If cosmographers like Roman used the name on their

maps of the Charlotte Harbor region, it is not improbable that the name runs back to the older Spanish period. Menendez established a mission on Charlotte Harbor in 1567. It lasted for only five years, but later many priests —Jesuit, Dominican and Franciscan—did their work in the region. Four of them bore the name of Gaspar and while the record is not definite any one of the four could have labored in the Charlotte Harbor field. On Little Gasparilla Key several ancient Spanish well-heads have been found. A mission may have been located on the key. One can imagine that the name of Gaspar or Gasparilla first came to Charlotte Harbor borne by some devoted priest. In the old records of one of these ancient orders the untold story of Friar Gaspar may still be buried, waiting to be found

Wherever fact lies, Gaspar still lives, pirate and roughneck, in the Pageant of Gasparilla, launched every spring by the socially exclusive Gasparilla Society of Tampa. Whatever his sins as a buccaneer and wherever he drove his corvette with its necklace of gleaming cannon mouths, he brings to a dour and confused world today, annually, three days of gaiety and honest laughter.

The other pirate records of the Mangrove Coast are few. There are some yarns about Black Caesar. Verrill, in his excellent "Romantic and Historic Florida," describes a piratical coaster by the name of Billy Bowlegs, who is said to have sunk a schooner, filled with treasure, in the shallow waters of a gulf coast bay within the last sixty years, and to have roosted hopefully near by for quite a time. This may all be so. No man knows his Florida romance better than Verrill.

But by and large the great stream of piracy and deep sea hijacking left the Mangrove Coast alone. There is sound reason for this. Piracy is eminently a business whose devotees are interested in the immediate dollar. There are no re-sales in piracy. To be a successful pirate you have to have a large body of uncertain and timorous merchantmen to attack. The commerce of the gulf in the tumultuous days from the crash of Napoleon to the 1830's was no great object. The thin but constantly expanding fleet that worked in and out of New Orleans, carrying cotton and sugar for the South and the bacon, hams, grain and timber that the rafts brought down the Ohio and Mississippi, were an important but still lesser note in world trade, compared to the fleet from all the great ports of the world that swept south to Rio and B. A. through the waters of the Bahamas and the Windward Passage to the East and the Florida Straits and the Yucatan Channel to the west. Like the buzzards of their favorite cities, the corsairs of the Caribbean hung close to the flanks of the great streams of commerce, the loot from which kept their murderous racket alive.

The general unsettlement following the Napoleonic wars turned a horde of privateers upon the commerce of the world. A wave of revolution swept the Spanish colonies from the Rio Grande to the Cape in the 'twenties. The rebellious governments were most reckless in issuing papers of marque and reprisal, and all this helped feed the growing fleets of pirates which flocked around Porto Rico and Cuba in the first two decades of the century. Officials of the Spanish colonial administration in Porto Rico and Havana were blatantly "in the racket." American war vessels chasing pirates were fired upon from Spanish batteries at San Juan in Porto Rico while Spanish governors of Cuba, as a rule, were most remiss at joining with the United States and Great Britain in clearing the Caribbean and the gulf of the pests. Off the Mole of St. Nicholas and off Cape Antonio, there were veritable nests of pirates, often as many as twenty or thirty at anchor at a time. No vessel dared make for the Yucatan Channel without facing an almost certain chase. The United States Navy was ordered to send a special fleet into the Caribbean in 1821. For a while it reported to Commodore Patterson at New Orleans. Later Key West, then called Thompson's Island in honor of Secretary of the Navy Smith Thompson, was made the base of the anti-piracy fleet under Commander David Porter. The *Lynx* and the *Nonesuch* cruised the Mangrove Coast from Key West and Havana to New Orleans while other vessels in the fleet concentrated on the eastern and western tips of Cuba. In September 1821, says the "Niles Register," American merchantmen were bagged off Cape

Antonio every week. For a time it was even worse than
that. There were days when as many as two and three
American vessels were taken and plundered. The crews
were often murdered and always terribly mistreated. In
one week in October 1821 the *Melita,* the *Leo,* the *Aristi-*
des, and the *Lucies* were taken off Cape Antonio. A week
before the brig *Clarissa* had been held up at the same
spot, while the schooner *Bold Commander* was taken a
little south of the Isle of Pines.

It was the capture of the *Lucies* that brought Lieutenant Lawrence Kearny in the *Enterprise* to Cape Antonio. Within a month he had captured and destroyed
four pirate schooners and one piratical sloop and set free
several captured American merchant vessels.

The year following witnessed an intensified drive
against the pirates of the Florida straits. The British
began a patrol about Jamaican waters and their sum-
mary justice to "privateers" off Gallows Hill beyond Port
Royale won them a sinister reputation with the buccaneering gentry. Congress sent the frigate *Macedonian*
south under the command of Captain Biddle, and with
it the frigate *Congress* and the sloops *Hornet, Peacock,*
Spark, Enterprise, Alligator, Shark, Porpoise and two
gunboats numbered 158 and 168, also the first steam
vessel in our navy—the converted steam ferry, the *Sea*
Gull. With this command, Biddle's men swept into every
bay and bight along the north coast of Cuba and on
along the coasts of Mexico, Central America and Co-

lombia. They had to fight not only pirates and the indifference of the Spanish officials but deadly epidemics of yellow fever. In fact, the naval station at Key West had to be abandoned in favor of Pensacola because of the regular visitations of the then utterly misunderstood plague.

Lafitte of New Orleans and Barataria fame was the only first-rate pirate the gulf coast ever produced, and he was the product of the looseness of the local governments in New Orleans which permitted him to dispose easily of stolen cargoes. He was helped, too, by the lack of any form of government along the Mexican-owned coast of Texas, rather than by his own talent.

Lafitte was more of a top muscle-man among the pirates than an actual cruising pirate. He "fenced" the merchandise brought in by pirates who outfitted at his post at Barataria and later at Galveston Island. When the American Navy drove him from these stations he disappeared. The legend is that he was along when Gasparilla sailed out to attack the *Enterprise* in that last and fatal raid, but inasmuch as that raid never took place—at least the *Enterprise* was not concerned—Lafitte may never have heard of Gasparilla. For many years there was the wreck of a schooner plainly visible on the bottom of the Manatee River below Bradenton. Oldsters used to say the vessel had belonged to Lafitte. Maybe it did. At one time he had under his general control quite a fleet of light draft vessels. But another story told along the Manatee River is that the black ribs of the old boat on the bottom of the river belonged to a flotilla of General Jackson's, carrying provisions to his army at Pensacola, and wrecked there by an untimely blow.

Loss of prestige and the wrecking of his organization forced Lafitte actually to go to sea under the black flag, and during 1822 he is reported at various places along the coast of Cuba actively engaged in his profession. He operated, whenever he could, as a privateer under the flag of Buenos Aires, Mexico or Colombia. It is said that he died in Yucatan in 1826 in the wind-up days of the racket, when American recognition of the infant South and Central American republics was, to a degree, stabilizing the waters of the Caribbean and the gulf, and when the American and British navies had done their part in setting the Caribbean in order.

Quite different from the pirates of the Cuban coast who, at their best, were a scurvy lot, were the tribe of international adventurers whose methods were brutal but who deserve a higher niche than the hijackers of commerce. Few of these touched the Mangrove Coast as there was richer and easier loot in the turbulent cities of revolutionary Latin America, then in the first stages of its revolt against Spain. But Sir George MacGregor for a moment in 1817 saw a chance to make Florida a "Spanish Republic." He had served with Wellington in the Peninsular Wars and later with Miranda and Bolivar. The weakness of the Spanish garrisons in Florida were

fully understood by him. He recruited his troops at
Charleston—about a thousand men—and after adventuring at Amelia Island on the East Coast for a time, announced his intention of transporting his men to Tampa
Bay. In West Florida he thought he saw an opportunity
of carving out a separate nation, with its capital on
Tampa Bay. He meant to extend his conquest as far
south as Charlotte Harbor, perhaps even to the Florida
keys, and move his lines as far to the north as he could
safely and easily drive the Indians back. Far removed
from the sharper international issues that loomed over
the waters of Bahama Straits, he felt that he would be
left alone to build his empire, his kingdom or his republic—for he wavered at times in his design—to establish a profitable trade with the Indians and to create an
international trade with Cuba and the West Indian islands by selling them smoked mullet in return for their
Spanish gold and European goods. It was a brave dream
while it lasted but MacGregor's financial backers had
another plan. There were opportunities galore in the
islands of the Caribbean. MacGregor marched his men
aboard his boats and sailed for Haiti. Making that island
his base of operations, he captured the islands of St. Andrews and Providence. The green cross flag of Florida
—MacGregor's own design—that was to have flown over
Tampa Bay fluttered instead over the indigo waters of
the harbor of old Providence. To his capital MacGregor
invited all of the scalawags and light-fingered gentry of

the explosive Caribbean, and to them—for a cash consideration plus a neat percentage of the potential swag —MacGregor, as a king among the kings, issued letters of marque and reprisal and gave a thin and ragged cloak of legality. The racket worked and MacGregor was strictly in the money but the old itch in his foot began again. The blue waves beckoned, and MacGregor with his crew made off for Porto Bello. He captured it, as it had been captured many times before by better and abler adventurers. But always the Scot, despite disease and desertion among his followers, he wangled a concession for fifty million acres along the Mosquito Coast of Nicaragua, and promptly entitled himself "His Highness Gregor, Cacique of Poyas." His light dimmed after that but twenty years later he was still alive, maintaining himself on his retirement pay as an officer of Bolivar's army.

Piracy on the gulf, along with piracy on the Caribbean, gave way slowly before the forces of law and order. The big marine insurance companies of Boston, New York and Philadelphia maintained a constant pressure on the government to keep the sea lanes safe for commerce. Piracy, like bootlegging a century later, lost its glamour; public opinion became fixed against it. The important centers for the "fencing" of stolen merchandise in New Orleans, Havana, San Juan, were closed. The surveillance of the American, British and, by this time, the Spanish navies became so effective that the risk became too great.

Yet as late as 1846 the citizens of Tampa petitioned the Federal government to send them some artillery and arms to equip a volunteer force against Mexican and Cuban privateers reported to be cruising in the gulf.

There were no Sir Henry Morgans, Dick Hawkinses, or Bartholomew Robertses in the buccaneering fleets of the period. Most of them were bedraggled crews who could dish it but not take it. Few died in bed; some came to their end by plunging overboard in the midst of a raid, to be welcomed by the tiger sharks and great hammer-heads attracted by the smell of blood, the story says, when such events took place, or stumbled up the gallows steps provided by the rough justice of the period.

Only one pirate known as Cofrecina had a touch of the old spirit. As he was approached by the executioner, who carried a black mask in one hand, he started back. "Take it away," he said. "Take it away. Inasmuch as I have seen three or four hundred people die by my own hand during my life, it would be most surprising if I did not know how to die."

SUNKEN CHESTS AND GOLD

DOUBLOONS

AND yet Spanish doubloons have been found and hidden chests have been located along the beaches of the Mangrove Coast.

The story of the treasure chest off Point o' Rocks, on Siesta Key, never dies, and at different times considerable sums have been spent in trying to find it.

Point o' Rocks is one of the highest points upon the long, low line of snow-white beach that extends from Sarasota Bay to Charlotte Harbor. It is the first landfall that coast-smart skippers aim to make when en route north from Key West to Tampa Bay. The earliest of the ancient Spanish charts mark it down and it was well known to the Miruelos and the other leading Spanish pilots of the exploring era. Siesta Key barricades the southern end of lovely Sarasota Bay, rising softly to a thirty-foot elevation at the "Point" and then shelving off again to the water's edge at Midnight Pass, which separates it from Venice shores and Treasure Island to the south.

119

For many years a narrow pass extended just below Point o' Rocks connecting the gulf with Sarasota Bay, but one night, during the great blow of 1921, the pass closed up, packed solid with gulf beach sand, and today there is no indication left, save a slight indentation called "Caples Cove," that the pass known on the old charts as "Rocky River" ever existed.

The big storm of '21 and the treasure chest are tied together. For it was on the afternoon before the storm that the chest was first discovered. Men who were on the boat and saw the chest still tell the tale.

A fishing party in a small cruiser was anchored off the pass, hand-lining for sheepshead and drums, when one of them noted something lying on the sea bottom some ten to twelve feet beneath them. Only a portion of it was visible, they will tell you, but enough to show two wide bands of iron running across the top with heavy iron clasps at the corners. Fishing for fish was immediately abandoned in favor of fishing for chests. Ropes were found aboard the boat and one of the men managed to dive to the bottom and get the rope around the chest several times. Tense with excitement, the men pulled with might and main. The big, bulky object slowly started upward. The box became more definite. It was, they say, about five feet long and two feet wide, and, as it approached the surface of the water, the iron work upon it became clear and more defined. The chest reached the surface, one corner indeed was in the air, when the rope broke and the prize slipped back. Again it lay on the sandy bottom of the gulf.

By this time the sun had set and the swift sub-tropical darkness swept across the waters. Marking the spot, the men reluctantly turned the boat's prow for home. The plan was to return at daybreak with heavier cable and adequate lifting apparatus to complete the job. Secrecy on the part of all hands was enjoined.

But the men did not come back the next morning. Nor for several mornings. For that night a terrific storm screamed over the gulf—the hurricane of '21—the pass closed up and the whole contour of the beach was changed. Eventually the men did come back, bringing their ropes and pulleys. They could not locate the chest but, believing that so heavy an object would not be far distant, they dove and dove and dove again without success. Then the story got out. Other men tried. Better apparatus was used but with no success. Finally in 1934 a mysterious group arrived, accompanied by several trucks, a gas engine and an air-pumping machine. They built a pier out into the water and set up the engine. Daily the diver appeared and went down into the water. Presently the strangers, who lived in a group of tents upon the beach, set out guards and allowed no one to approach near enough to see what was taking place. But one night, near-by residents say, the gas engine ran on until late in the evening and men could be seen working on some sort of an object at the end of the pier. About midnight there was a considerable commotion around the camp. The engines on the trucks began to growl. The tents came down, the machinery was loaded and long before daylight the entire party had disappeared. Nothing but the long narrow pier remained for the wondering and the curious to stare at. Then a tough blow came out of the north and blew even that to bits.

But real gold has been often found on the Mangrove Coast, gold that you could see and touch. Gold that you could bite and spend. Spanish gold—perhaps pirates' gold.

"Alligator" Ferguson, for instance, had some. There were either a number of "Alligator" Fergusons up and down the Mangrove Coast at various times, or "Alligator" lived to a ripe old age and traveled a great deal, for you will find guides talking of "Alligator" Ferguson and his activities south of the Shark, and again you will hear of an "Alligator" Ferguson busy along the beach as far north as Cedar Keys. This "Alligator" Ferguson worked the keys and rivers between Tampa Bay and Charlotte Harbor and, at times, had a hut that he lived in during the mullet season on Longboat Key. "Alligator" Ferguson, they say, knew a lot about Spanish treasure—much more than he would tell. When "Alligator" was not down on the Miakka marshes chasing the 'gators for their hides, he made his living fishing and crabbing along Siesta Key and its neighbors, St. Armands and Longboat.

In the early 'nineties, however, "Alligator" dropped his usual trips after the 'gators. He was, he said, getting too old to hang safely on to their terrific tails. Besides, he said, he had other means. And to one or two of his cronies he showed a handful of gold coins. On another occasion and rather more freely, he displayed a badly damaged old wheel-lock pistol. Queried as to where he found it, he said he'd picked it up on the Longboat beach.

Then "Alligator" began going to a Tampa bank. The first time he appeared, the story goes, was on a summer day in the early 'nineties, and after some hesitation, he disclosed a small pile of gold coins and asked what they were worth. The banker, anxious to help him, wired a collector in New York, and as the coins were dated about the middle of the eighteenth century, he secured a price somewhat above their market value as gold. Several times that summer the strange figure of the old man appeared at the bank. Each time he had a small heap of coins. In all he sold around eighteen hundred dollars' worth of gold coin during the year. He consistently refused to tell where he found the coins.

There have been plenty of wrecks along Siesta, Longboat and Anna Maria Keys, and occasionally a hulk of one of the old vessels will turn up whose history is utterly unknown. Such a wreck was discovered by William Whipple of Siesta Key in 1925 while excavating for a canal. This was the hull of what must have been a primitive steamer as it still had the remains of a single cylinder steam engine in it. A few coins of about 1840 were found but no treasure. The interesting thing about this wreck was that it was found at least a half mile from the present line of the beach. Another, found more recently at the very end of Longboat Key, has been only partially excavated. It appears to be a much older vessel and may even be of the Spanish colonial period.

At the mouth of the Peace, as it flows into the Caloosahatchee and Charlotte Harbor, the fishermen will tell you that if the tide is right and the water clear, you can see the remains of three old cannon.

"I heard tell," said one of them, "that the Spanish used to fill the barrels of their cannon with gold money and then they tossed them overboard for safe keeping. Some of us tried to lift one of the cannon once but we didn't have the tackle. Couldn't budge it."

The entire coast from Tampa Bay to the Caloosahatchee abounds with Indian mounds, Indian fields and Spanish "sign."

"We found six Spaniards once when I was a youngster," said a guide to me one afternoon. "A bunch of us kids were down around Punta Rassa and up a creek bed we found a funny looking mound. We thought it was Indian and we got a spade and went after it. The mound wasn't a deep one and we turned up some skeletons pretty quick. But they wasn't Indians. They were Spanish."

"How did you know they were Spanish?" I asked.

"Oh," he said, "they had their bones all wrapped up in some old pieces of black plush. They had leather boots on, too. One of the boys said he guessed they all died of yellow jack so we threw the dirt back on pretty quick and got out of there. But they didn't have any money around 'em, for I looked."

Just south of Sarasota along the bay front a search for buried Spanish treasure took place some years ago. A beautiful grove of live oak stands on the spot and for years children playing about the grove occasionally brought home pieces of old iron, copper medals and coins. One evening lights were noted at the place by passing motorists and the next day a large hole was discovered. Apparently a large chest had been taken out. A few copper and silver coins were found scattered about the hole but no one ever found out who dug the hole or what was taken away.

The slave trade had a part in the piratical activities of the decades following the collapse of France. One of the reasons for the dislike of Americans on the part of Spanish officials of the West Indian colonies was the fact that America had outlawed the slave trade in 1807 and had thus destroyed a hugely profitable business in the Spanish colonies which, until then, had been the principal way-stations for the African slavers en route to America. The slavers not only utilized the Spanish islands to clean and fatten up their cargo, but many disposed of their

blacks in Havana, San Juan and Matanzas to be re-sold
to American importers later by the Cuban factors. The
prohibition of the traffic by the American government
destroyed this profitable business as a legal institution
but it did not destroy the trade. Part of the work of the
American naval anti-piracy squadron was in overhauling
slavers attempting to run cargoes into the hidden bays
of the Florida gulf coast. Once inside these lonely bays,
Negroes could be landed and turned over to those appointed to receive them and, if not sold immediately to
American planters, could be marched north and slipped
into Georgia, Alabama and Mississippi for further disposition. A sound Negro brought from three hundred
dollars to four hundred dollars in cash on the beach and
a shipment of a few hundred slaves brought a price worth
reaching for. Many a cargo was landed on the long
beaches between Pensacola and Cedar Keys and as far
south as Tampa Bay, and then marched, safari style, into
southern Georgia.

Captures were frequent. Negroes found aboard the
slavers were taken to Key West, where large and well-
built camps had been constructed and there, following
adjudication, the Negroes were generally shipped to Jamaica where they could obtain employment as freemen.
Great Britain had outlawed slavery in her West Indian
colonies, causing great heart-burning in the South, where
it was argued that the Negroes were virtually treated as
slaves anyhow. The problem of the disposal of the freed

slaves was not an easy one. The laws of the country and public sentiment in the South prevented their being brought into America and permitted to seek a livelihood as freemen. They could not be returned to the Congo country, for in that case, they would be immediately recaptured and probably resold into a slavery infinitely more brutal than any ever conceived of in the United States. The British West Indies seemed to be the only outlet and to the British many of them went. Later the Negro colony of Liberia, in Africa, received many of the captured slave cargoes.

As the years went on and the slave stock in the South was threatened with exhaustion, the prices on bootlegged slaves went higher and the efforts to run them through increased. This brought about an inevitable increase in captures by the patrolling naval vessels and on one occasion in the late 'fifties, it is said, there were over twelve hundred freed captives awaiting disposition in the government quarters at Key West. The government took excellent care of its charges. One part of the pens was reserved for women and children and another for the men. The pens were cleaned daily, whitewashed frequently and special bathing accommodations were provided, and officials saw to it that they were used. Antislavery societies in the North kept a benevolent eye over them and provided them with some amusements. The government looked after the captives' health and they probably ate better than at any time in their lives. The

"Weekly Peninsula" of Tampa reported a dramatic incident in which a Negro woman, brought to Key West from
a captured African slaver, discovered in an adjoining
compound her husband and two sons, captured in the
same raid on a Congo village in Africa but separated in
the slave pens of the Gold Coast and brought to America
in different boats. They were reunited and sent to Jamaica together.

The coves and bays of the Mangrove Coast played
their old part again in the rum-running industry during
the piping times of prohibition and hundreds of cargoes
of illicit liquor were taken aboard at Bimini and Havana
in fast, light draft boats, and brought ashore at the innumerable landing spots among the sheltered keys. Here
they would be met by trucks; the burlap bags, each con-
taining a half-dozen bottles, would be hurried ashore,
loaded on the trucks and rushed northward to Tampa
and the north for retail distribution.

The Coast Guards did their best but the odds against
them were terrific. The population, generally speaking,
were not very interested in the enforcement of the prohibition laws; many of the men engaged were local citizens, and the Coast Guard got less than co-operation
from the folks on shore.

Repeal ended all that, although now and then an occasional cargo of Havana rum is still slipped in among
the keys for local distribution. Today the risky water

trade is in running Chinamen, European refugees without visas, and drugs. Nothing like the big days of rum-running, yet a sizable, illegal game. Human freight and drugs are landed fairly regularly on isolated gulf coast beaches.

Headquarters of these ventures are in Havana and New York. Six hundred dollars per head is the usual charge for landing an illegal immigrant. The Cuban operators use small sailing vessels and, working north across the Gulf, seek a hiding place north of the Shark and then, sailing by night through the hidden channels of the Ten Thousand Islands, attempt to contact their American agents on one of the keys off Charlotte Harbor or in Sarasota Bay. The cargo, human and otherwise, is taken by auto to some inland city where it will be less conspicuous, to entrain for northern destinations. The new trade is doubly dangerous for all concerned. The Coast Guard patrol has to be evaded, and more than once it has been known to happen that the crew, finding itself in danger, has knocked their passengers on the heads and dumped the bodies overboard to escape detection and arrest. Drug-running is a little simpler. Cuban fishing schooners run far north into the gulf at every season of the year following the great schools of kingfish and mullet. A few miles off shore it is exceedingly easy for smugglers operating speedboats to move out in the dusk, take over the comparatively small, compact packages, and get to shore without detection.

CHAPTER II

THE BANNERS PASS

IT was July 17, 1821. Through the night heavy squalls swept over Pensacola. As the dawn was breaking, black clouds again piled up in the south and for an hour the heavy sheets of tumbling water thudded relentlessly upon the dull, red tiles and the mossy cypress shingles of the city's roofs. The rain slashed across the shuttered front of the Government House upon the Plaza where slept Jose Callava, last of the Spanish governors of West Florida. It splattered into futile mist against the tall, two-galleried house on the other side of the unkempt plaza where Rachel Jackson rested awaiting the arrival of the General in the morning. It beat upon the white sand of the Plaza, whipping it up until it covered the struggling wire grass and formed in gleaming pools where the ragged paths bisected it. Below the Plaza the water rose between the muddy curbs until the streets ran knee-high. The early storm-bound workers huddled for refuge under the live oaks.

The tall clock in the hallway of the Government House

registered with each sixty seconds the passing of the two hundred and eighty-eight years of the rule of Spain over the Floridas. A dozen Spanish kings and queens (and for an interlude of twenty years a British sovereign) had held the royal colony and molded it to suit the royal whims. Thirty-six popes, from their austere offices in the far-off Vatican, had held spiritual domination over the colony and through devoted Jesuit, Franciscan and Dominican fathers had sought to expand among Indians and newcomers an understanding of the seven deadly sins and the spiritual and corporeal works of mercy. Tall Ponce de Leon, red-bearded Narváez, hot-eyed and eager De Soto, Pedro Menendez de Aviles, Fray Luis Cancer and countless others had died violently, or suffered disaster or shattered health, all to increase the royal wealth and power, and to raise high the banner of the Christian God. For three hundred and eight years the shadow of Spain, of England and of France had lain over the colonies of the Floridas.

The clock ticked on; the drumbeat of the marching rain died away to a whispering drizzle. A soldier stepped out from a sentry box, attached the flag of Spain to the high flagpost in the center of the Plaza and slowly ran it to the top where it drooped in lifeless folds in the humid morning air.

At seven o'clock Betty, Rachel Jackson's ebullient light brown maid, looking out upon the upper gallery and the Plaza, reported to her mistress, who was busily getting into her brocaded overskirt, that twenty dismounted dragoons of the Tarragona regiment, in "elegant attire" were stiffly stretched across the front of the Government House.

At eight o'clock a battalion of the Fourth Regiment, United States Infantry, under Colonel Brooke, and a company of the Fourth United States Artillery, swung into the square. They marched across the Plaza, faced about and came to rest. The Americans had slept at Galvez Springs, two miles away, where Jackson had maintained his last headquarters, and had had to splash their way into the city. Major Dinkins, with four companies of infantry, was ordered to Fort Barrancas to proceed with the ceremonies incident to taking over.

General Andrew Jackson was now due. Despite his long stay at Manuels and Galvez Springs, despite invitation and suggestion, the General and the Governor had not met. Punctilio had fought with protocol, misunderstanding with mistranslation, dyspepsia with diplomacy, and throughout the long and dusty road from New Orleans, where Jackson had arrived late in April from Nashville, until he had reached Galvez Springs, three days before, the General and the Governor had worn each other's patience thin in long epistolary exchanges.

Up to the very last, the General did try to arrange a meeting. On Sunday evening, July 15th, Jackson had written Dr. Bronaugh, who had gone ahead with Rachel

Jackson into Pensacola, of his intention to invite the Governor to breakfast, and urged his co-operation.

"The Scripture," wrote the General, "says to return good for evil and in this feeling I am asking the Governor and his secretaries to dine with me; he is, I suppose, very sore." But the Governor, in a cloud of compliments, evaded the breakfast.

The General had not slept for the past two nights. He worked at his papers and correspondence until long after midnight. The mosquitoes swarmed into his rooms at Galvez Springs and fairly ate him up.

Worse than mosquitoes, red bugs and chiggers had bitten the General on his trip from New Orleans to his first stop at Montpelier. He had lingered there for weeks, and then went on to Manuels, Florida, fifteen miles from Pensacola, where he had had to wait another month before going into Galvez Springs. Rachel had been with him, which was a comfort, and Dr. J. C. Bronaugh, Surgeon-General for the Southern District, and Judge Henry M. Breckenridge. His personal aide and nephew, Lieut. Andrew J. Donelson, had been invaluable. The little group devoted themselves to protecting the General from the incessant onslaughts of admirers, place-seekers and politicians; from the attacks of his recurrent "bowel trouble" and from his own burning rages that swept over him with cyclonic force, and at times threatened to engulf the whole expedition in fury and disaster.

There had been delay from the very start, unexplainable to the General, who wished speed and dispatch above all things. In New Orleans, the General had been thrown into a paroxysm of anger because the New Orleans banks refused to take his draft against the United States Treasury for troop and expedition expenses, except at a tremendous discount. It took over a month before he received four thousand seven hundred and twenty dollars from Colonel Gadsden against drafts sold at a figure to the General's satisfaction. Then there was the matter of Colonel James Forbes. At about the time the General left Nashville, Colonel Forbes had left New York in the naval sloop, *Hornet,* to secure the necessary signature of the Captain General of Havana to the papers authorizing the governors of West and East Florida to transfer the territory to the United States. A simple assignment at the time, it had seemed. The *Hornet* reached Havana in good time, but from the hour the trim little sloop slipped past Morro Castle for her berth on the Regla side, Colonel Forbes' mission bogged down in a fog of postponement, misadventure and delay. The Captain-General was ill; the Captain-General had been called away; the Captain-General would see the Colonel shortly. A whole month passed before Colonel Forbes was able to present his credentials to the Spanish governor. Rumors meantime were flying thick and fast along the waterfront of New Orleans, Mobile, St. Augustine and Savannah. The big Havana exporting houses were utilizing every day's delay to dump additional cargoes into Florida. The Spanish merchants of Pensacola and St. Augustine for years had enjoyed a practical monopoly of the retail trade of the colony. They intended to fight hard to retain their old supremacy. They were filling up their warehouses to bursting with Spanish goods, bought cheaply on long credits.

More sinister rumors reached Jackson. Cuba was a center for the slave trade in the western hemisphere, and since the prohibition of the importation of slaves into the United States in 1807, Cuba had become the natural depot for African slavers who schemed to run their cargoes into the South. Anyhow, Florida under Spanish control was an attractive base of operations for human merchandise on its way into Georgia, South Carolina and the booming cotton states of Alabama and Mississippi.

The Spanish slave dealers, Jackson knew, were utilizing every day of the delay to land blacks in the colony. Always a hater of the "trade," Jackson wrote Commodore Patterson, United States Navy, at New Orleans, urging that American warships be sent as far south as Tampa Bay to prevent such importation. He turned his own attention to affairs within the territory. There were several Americans in jail in Pensacola and the General was informed that the Spanish meant to take these unfortunates to Havana for further punishment.

Always deeply suspicious of the Spanish—likewise the British—the General wrote to Governor Cavalla. The Governor promptly replied that there were no Americans in Pensacola jails. Not satisfied, General Jackson informed Cavalla tartly that no Americans would be allowed to leave Pensacola with the Spanish troops.

"I hear," he wrote, "that the Spanish are tearing down houses belonging to absent Americans and using the wood for fuel."

The transportation of American soldiers from Mobile and New Orleans to Pensacola took an amount of arranging. Apparently there were endless matters to write about to the Spanish governor; for instance the matter of the Spanish cannon at Fort Barrancas. Governor Cavalla wrote that he could not surrender the cannon with the forts; no provision, he said, had been made for the sacrifice of munitions, only of the forts themselves. Jackson's pen scratched long and fiercely over that one before the Governor accepted the Jacksonian position. There was the matter of rations for the Spanish troops, to be taken on the two schooners, to be escorted by the *Hornet* to Havana. How much white bread; how much hard bread; how many sacks of beans and how much fish? The *Ann Martin* and the *Tom Shields* had been chartered in New Orleans, to carry the soldiers. The *Hornet* would take most of the officers and their wives. In all, six hundred and thirty-one men were to be repatriated, including eleven wives, twenty-two children and seventy slaves. Many nice points of social and military distinction had to be cared for. The messengers from Montpelier galloped along the dusty road to Pensacola to meet others from Pensacola en route to Montpelier. The words ran to thousands.

Despite the hospitality of the Alabama planters, it had been dull for Rachel at Montpelier. June came with the news that Colonel Forbes and the *Hornet* had at last arrived at Pensacola with the Captain-General's signature on the papers. The General, Rachel, secretaries, advisers, interpreters and staff hurriedly packed and posted away to Manuels. They reached there on June 15th, hopeful that formalities would soon be over. The General reckoned without his Spanish opponent. Days went by at Manuels; the same story as at Montpelier. Rachel, with most of the staff, including Lieutenant Donelson, moved on and took possession of the big house in town. The General was left alone with his stomach spasms, the midges and mosquitoes, and the interminable correspondence with Governor Cavalla. Minor irritations mounted. Betty, Rachel's maid, had been having something like a social triumph of her own among the bucks of Pensacola. Rachel had cause for grave displeasure.

Amid the long drawn out negotiations with Cavalla over details of the transference of the flags, the General had time to spare to vent his displeasure on anyone who caused the slightest trouble to his Rachel. He wrote on to Donelson at once that the maid Betty "was putting on airs and has been guilty of impudence. She can behave herself if she will. . . . I have told her that publicly whipped she shall be." The General recommended fifty lashes.

Finally July 17th was the date set for the ceremonies at Government House and also at Fort Barrancas. At seven-thirty of that cloudy July morning, Colonel George Brooke, with the band in front and colors flying, led the American troops into the Plaza.

The General, walking just a trifle stiffly, called for his horse. The entire American party galloped up the street and into the Plaza. They halted before the saluting soldiers. Jackson, in full dress, every one of the nine bands of glittering gold braid topped by a large gold button, his heavy golden epaulets gleaming, raised his low, cockaded hat to Rachel. She and her party were on the upper gallery of the house. He tossed back a rebellious cowlick and dismounted carefully, threw a stern glance down the long line of waiting troops and stalked into his house.

"How solemn was his countenance when he dismounted from his horse," wrote Rachel in a letter later to a Nashville friend.

Almost at once Jackson and his party left the house again and walked briskly across the Plaza between the Spanish and the American soldiers. At the gateway the Spanish sentries presented arms and the big door opened. The few formalities were quickly over. The

Spanish guard in front of the Governor's house was called
to attention, and marched away. American soldiers took
their places. The big doors of the Government House
again opened and Jackson, accompanied by Cavalla,
walked back across the Plaza to Jackson's house when
the brief official visit was over. As Cavalla reappeared,
the Spanish flag came slowly down; the American flag
went up, "full one hundred feet." The Spanish troops followed with the departing Governor. The band broke into
"The Star-Spangled Banner" and the guns on the *Hornet*
boomed.

The citizens of Pensacola, most of whom were Spanish, watched the scene in silence.

Rachel Jackson saw it all from the upper gallery.
"Many burst into tears," she wrote. "I have never seen
so many pale faces." Yet, good, sound Presbyterian
that she was, she felt that God's hand was in it also.
"They were living far from God," she wrote. "The field
is white for the harvest. Oh for one of our faithful ministers to come and impart the word of life to them."

At that, Rachel's eyes were not entirely shut to the
church which had monopolized the business of souls
during the years of the Spanish rule. "There is a Cath-
olic church in the place," wrote Rachel later, "and the
priest seems a divine looking man. He comes to see us
and he dined with us yesterday." She was profoundly
shocked, however, at the easy recreational Sunday of
the Spaniard with its occasional cockfight, horse race

or fandango. Its casual acceptance of gambling stirred
her deeply. "What a heathen land I am in," she wrote.
"Never but once have I heard a Gospel sermon nor has
the song of Zion sounded in my ears."

For the third time the General was seeing the American emblem flutter from the flag posts of Pensacola.
This time it was no temporary raid. Shaking loose from
the crowd of job-hunting, favor-seeking Americans who
were in Pensacola to witness the transfer, he gathered
up Breckenridge and Bronaugh and retired to his office.

A brief letter was drafted to the President to notify
him of the completion of the ceremony. Then the proclamations, drafted by the three men during the hot,
still afternoons at Montpelier and at Manuels, were
brought out. Proclamations to consolidate Florida into
a single territory; proclamations to revise and improve
municipal government; proclamations to provide for an
extension and increase in certain taxes, and proclamations giving municipal officials the power to close all
places deemed offensive to them, be they gambling hells
or churches. Rachel was to have her Christian Sabbath.
The proclamations fell softly to the floor to be gathered
up by Breckenridge, appointed Alcalde of Pensacola,
and prepared for publication. The General stared mood-
ily across the desk.

"It's a goose chasing expedition," he wrote the next
day. "The policing is wretched. The whole town is in-

undated. It has rained for two months. If I can get home with a loss less than all my emoluments of one thousand dollars, I will be contented."

This was July. By November 3rd, after a tempestuous summer in Pensacola, he was back at the Hermitage. Rachel hoped it would be forever. But Coffee, Campbell and Carroll were already writing about the Presidency.

There is a curious and arresting vitality about the Spanish. Short-visioned economist, somnolent colonial administrator, endowed with an infinite capacity for leisure; yet, wherever the Spaniard has lodged himself, established his people and implanted his ways and processes of thought for a time, regardless of what great changes take place, what new systems and ideas crowd in to supplant his will and method, in architecture, culture and cuisine, the imprint of the Spaniard will remain.

So it was in Pensacola. The great striped banner of blood and gold had gone. So had the soldiers and their officers with their feathered hats, snug blouses and long, tight, white-buttoned trousers. Governor Jose Cavalla lingered on until he crashed headlong into one of Jackson's moods of dyspeptic irritation and was arrested and imprisoned. Cavalla accepted the diplomatic outrage with rare unconcern, gathered the remnants of his staff about his cell, called for champagne and guitars, and astonished the choleric Tennesseean with an exhibition of how a sophisticated Spanish gentleman takes a night in jail. Officially Spain had retreated to Havana, but hundreds of Spaniards stayed on. The Merenos, Bonifays, Gonzales, Sierras and de la Ruas were active factors in the city's life for decades to come, competing valiantly with the Brosnahans, the Jerrisons, Campbells and Chases for political and commercial honors. The records of the town from 1821 to the Civil War show plainly its cosmopolitan character. The Spanish were there, and the Irish. Numbers of Americans had come in with the flag, keen eyed, eager fingered and strictly on the make. There were a scattering of Germans and of Portuguese and numerous French émigrés from the Santo Domingo slave revolt. They fled to Pensacola from Louisiana in a futile effort to escape the sweeping expansion of the Protestant, republican American nation.

It took time to change the slow and lazy ways that had dominated the community for a century and a half. Trading, though often brisk, was primitive.

"Jose," said a shopkeeper one day soon after the American occupation, "when are you going to pay me for that cheese?"

"Cheese," replied Jose. "I don't owe you for a cheese. But I do owe you for a grindstone."

"Grindstone," said the shopkeeper. "Wait a minute. Let me look at my books again. Grindstone, that's it. I forgot to put a hole in the picture of that cheese."

At one time there had been a good deal of indigo shipped out of the port but cotton was gradually replacing all other staples. The American newcomers found that in cotton, timber, naval stores and land lay their best chances for profit.

The twin scourges of Real Estate Boom and Yellow Jack shook the town as soon as the flags had been transferred. Inflated values on city lots crashed in the panic that came as the yellow fever broke. Many of the Americans fled, never to return. Those who stayed were due to suffer many other booms and more assaults of fever. Whatever disaster happened, Pensacola lived and grew. But the hand of Spain rests on it to this day.

CHAPTER 12

BUT THREE CAME BACK

THE NEW YEAR high jinks of 1835 had barely quieted down before Washington heard again from Thompson at Fort King. In the stuffy, low-ceilinged offices of the War Department, there was no taste for the dispatches always coming up from Florida, and always bringing bad news. General Wiley Thompson at Fort King was worrying again. Treaties were nothing to the Seminoles. They showed no intention of giving up their Florida lands as agreed, or selling their cattle, disposing of their Negroes, and taking off for the lands allotted them west of the Mississippi.

The White House, too, had no taste for the sixes and sevens described in dispatches. Cotton was selling well enough, true; western real estate was moving with a briskness that even to the Old General seemed fantastic. Canals were dug and towns laid out so fast the pioneers were out of breath. Money bulged out of every bank window, or so it seemed. But the abolitionists never stopped their clamor; the tariff was still a fighting word; the news from Texas looked black.

Andy Jackson, tired and looking forward to the Hermitage, roused himself when Thompson's dispatches were brought in to him. The Seminoles again. What did their chiefs call themselves now? Micanopy—Alligator—Wild Cat—the same old panther litter.

"All bastard Creeks," he muttered. "I'll send them a message through Thompson."

His hand moved heavily across the paper.

"You know me," he wrote, "and I would not deceive you. I tell you that you must go. You have sold your land. You have not a place as big as a blanket to sit upon."

Andrew Jackson had won the first Seminole war for the United States. That was in 1818, the year before Spain ceded Florida to the United States. Jackson heartily believed that the only good Indians were dead ones, and at times he did not hesitate to add the British and Spanish to his list. He had crossed the border and marched hundreds of miles east and west in the Spanish colony, raiding Indian encampments, seizing and hanging British Indian traders whom he suspected, and probably rightly, of inciting the Indians against the interests of his country. As a final fillip to his campaign, he marched his troops into the friendly and loyal city of Pensacola and occupied its forts with American soldiers.

His whirlwind march upset the Spanish, but it did for the time settle the Indian question on the Florida frontier. Jackson had been the first American general to meet the Seminoles. Many other American generals met them later, a long and bedraggled list of them, but none ever understood Indian fighting in the South as did Jackson; none had his dash and not one approximated his success. Jackson finished the Florida campaign in the first Seminole war in four months. The wars that followed lasted over twenty years and cost a million dollars per year. It took eighty-two years to May, 1938 before the chiefs of the Florida Seminoles formally met with officials of the United States government and agreed upon a "peace." In terms of years, it was easily America's longest war, and until the Civil War it was one of the most expensive.

Slave owners, interested in eliminating Seminole camps in Florida as safe havens for their runaway stock, cattle men who saw in the green ranges of central Florida the promise of a great cattle land, and land-hungry planters all had a hand in the second and the continuing Seminole wars. The game was to hold conferences with the Indians, befuddle them with whisky, or frankly bribe them to sign treaties undertaking to move their clans west to lands in what is now Oklahoma and Texas. The Indians in the villages repudiated the "treaties," and American generals, on their side, often went back on their promises to the chiefs. In the bitter disputes that followed, the solemn contracts of both

tribe and nation were ripped to bits and the torn frag-
ments fluttered about as futilely as dead leaves before
the autumn wind. Political Washington, pressured by
the slave interests and served by military opinion based
on Jackson's apparently easy march of 1818, grossly
underestimated the difficult terrain and the ability and
intelligence with which the Indians would fight. British
traders from the Bahamas, scenting an attractive penny,
busily supplied the Seminoles with munitions whenever
the Indians had money or goods. The 'Glades were almost impenetrable to the regular soldiers and far from
attractive to the volunteer troops.

The big gates of the stockade flew open. The pipes
and drums of the barracks corps squealed and thumped.
The troops marched out—one hundred two men and
eight commissioned officers—and the thin line of marching bayonets streamed down the rough, uneven trail
leading from Fort Brooke on Tampa Bay to Fort King,
one hundred miles to the north and east. The great gates
closed. The men moved on. The pale winter sun barely
warmed the chill winter dampness. The trill of the pipes
became fainter and fainter. Major Dade, at the head of
his column, was not sure whether his ears really caught
the tune. The dark line twisted around a cypress sink
and disappeared behind the trees. It was the day before
Christmas, 1835.

The officers of the little detachment began to feel

better. Four days out from Fort Brooke, there had been "signs" of Indians but they had seen none. The construction of a primitive bridge on the north fork of the Withlacoochee had slowed things up. The heavy oxen, hauling the baggage wagons and the one six-pounder, had delayed things too, but with a good deal of pulling and hauling the entire lot had got safely across. The trail was a feeble path but clear. Each day the scouts, sent out on both flanks, came back with "nothing to report." Louis, the colored guide loaned to Major Dade at Fort Brooke because he spoke the Seminole tongue and knew the country, seemed to be sure they would see no Indians at all north of the Withlacoochee. Apparently the worst of the trip was over. Dade told the men that as his troop lined up for the day's march.

"Men," he said, "you have had hard going. But we are over the worst of it. With luck we may reach Fort King tonight."

If the blithering cold would only let up, what Louis called a "northerner"! It had been chilly the morning they left Fort Brooke; by evening the wind had the men, in their thin Key West issue uniforms, blue with the cold. Sloshing through the high grass, top-heavy with dew, the men were soaked in no time and their hands were so stiff they could barely hang on to their rifles.

The Irish in the ranks kept the line from going "sour." A third of the detachment came from Limerick, Mayo, Sligo and Antrim, and the jokes and songs did by day what the stiff issue of rum did for the men each evening.

But the grass grew high on either side of the trail and the seed-laden tops on the brown stalks glittered as the dew drops tossed back the sunlight. The forest stood well back from the trail. Dade contented himself with a small advance guard instead of the usual contingent of scouts on his flanks. The men marched at route step, in irregular order, some two by two, others in single file, stretching for a couple of hundred yards. In the rear were the baggage wagons headed by the old six-pounder drawn by a straining double team of oxen.

The Major was well ahead. Fifty yards behind him rode Captain U. S. Fraser of the Third Artillery and behind him Lieutenant R. R. Mudge. The men had their overcoats buttoned tight about them with their ammunition boxes beneath their jackets. Nearly all had their arms folded about their guns and their hands drawn up into their sleeves, to keep warm and to keep the dew on the high grass out of their faces. The irregular line had been moving for well on two hours. Captain Fraser, a small man on a big horse, had turned around to call out something to Mudge about freezing his feet in a footbath on horseback in a jungle in the sunny south. Mudge laughed. As he laughed came the screech of the Seminole war cry. It seemed to come from under Fraser's horse. A single shot rang out and the Captain saw his Major crumple off his mount and pitch forward.

"The sonsabitches," he shouted. "They got Dade."

The two officers went tearing back through the high brown grass to their men.

In the tall grass two hundred Seminoles shivered in the cold wind. Micanopy had kept the braves dancing throughout the night, without a fire, in a close-packed circle, chanting as they stamped round and round. Their Negro slaves, camp followers and allies shuffled and patted their hands as the dancers circled, stirring their own blood and making a rhythm to take the place of the silenced drums. Micanopy's plan was simple. Alligator's men were to hold the center. Jumper was to be on his right. Micanopy would take the left flank. He had a reason for that. His scouts, who had been in constant contact with Dade's men from the time they had left Fort Brooke, had reported how Dade rode ahead of his troops just behind the advance guard. Micanopy had explained to the council on the evening before that day, how he would shoot first, when Jumper gave the war cry. He would kill Dade. To do this he must be on the left.

It had been hard holding in the braves the night before while Dade's men were rebuilding the ruined bridge. But Dade had first built a heavy log defense about the center of his camp and he had men out on all sides. Still the Seminoles might have overwhelmed the soldiers in a first rush but some might have remained alive to put up fierce battle behind the log barrier. The six-pounder, Micanopy reflected, might do tremendous execution. He wanted to start his fight with the six-pounder out of action. That was why he decided to meet the soldiers in the tall grass where they could be confused by their hidden attackers.

Micanopy could hear the soldiers coming. He peeped through the wild oats and saw the advance guard across the gleaming grass. Behind them, riding clear of the protecting shrubbery, was Dade, squinting at the sun, his hands on his saddle horn. Slowly Micanopy elevated his rifle. Down the long, sharply defined defile of his rifle sights the officer loomed large and clear. The sun shone on his gold coat buttons. Micanopy brought his rifle barrel to a steady level.

Jumper shrilled the war cry. Micanopy's arm froze to the rifle shaft and he pressed the trigger.

The first volley from the Indians killed all the oxen. The great animals pulling the six pounder lay sunk down as if asleep. Two or three of the men managed to pull out of their overcoats and answered the Indians' fire from behind some small trees. Lieutenant Mudge dropped in an early blast. Captain Fraser fell close by. Captains Gardiner and Basinger ran to the six-pounder. Surgeon Gatlin was down in the grass by a wounded soldier. Captain Henderson lay dead, his body across the trail where he had dropped at that terrible first volley. The men had the six-pounder loaded but Basinger fell as he was touching off the fuse. A soldier took over and the six-pounder roared. The clamor of the yelping Indians was stilled for an instant, then, mixed with the whine of their rifle balls, the sound became higher and fiercer. The six-pounder boomed again. Only three men were left on the gun now. One of them fell. The other two rammed home a charge—one more boom. Then the yelping died away and the fire from the Indians seemed to lessen.

Captain Gardiner seized the opportunity. Rallying his men, he handed out axes from one of the wagons. The men went at some trees. The trunks, with limbs still attached, were hastily pulled together to form a rough "V" shaped enclosure around the big gun, with the open end facing the narrow marsh beyond which the Seminoles were gathered. The bodies of Basinger and Henderson were pulled inside the slender barricade.

"We can hold the devils off yet," Gardiner said, as he swung his sabre. The flash of the steel caught the eye of a Seminole sharpshooter and Gardiner sank to the ground.

The soldiers closed in about the gun and crouched behind the brush and log breastworks. As Gardiner keeled over, the Indians resumed their heavy firing. Gardiner's men could see them coming closer from behind trees and then leaping forward from one tree to another. The soldiers returned the fire coolly but their ammunition was growing scarce. And steadily they could see the Indians pressing on, coming, always coming closer, always in greater numbers.

Only three men came back, Thomas, Sprague and Clarke; all terribly wounded. It was Clarke alone who was able to give any connected account of the disaster. It was the worst defeat that the United States regular army had ever met at the hands of Indians up to that date.

The Seminole war dragged on. The old Indian fighter in the White House was there no more. The sleek Van Buren, with only a Broadway acquaintance with Indians, and the Tammany tribe at that, was in his place to hold down the lonely job in Washington. With the national banking system almost submerged, with a sound currency practically non-existent, with foreign money-lenders, in frantic anxiety, squeezing the pulp of American enterprises in a dim hope that, by pressure alone, they might extract gold, the larger proportion of the President's visitors had been worried and distracted men who hoped without hope that the Magical Van might be able to produce some sort of a financial rabbit out of the high beaver hats of the Treasury and thus save the business structure of the country.

But that hope was vain. The political wizard of the Hudson River valley was of no adventuring mind in the highways and the alleys of finance. The conception of governmental interference with the fixed laws controlling the ebb and flow of prosperity would have to wait another hundred years and for another Hudson River valley politician, before an impious governmental hand would hurl a stone at the high altars of approved economics.

And in and above the pleas and pressures of ruined merchants and starving workers, came the dull throb of the drum-beats from the swamps of Florida; more men —more money—more money—more men. With a tax-sensitive public clamoring for the reduction of national expense, the solemn generals from the War Department grouped about the big rosewood desk in the White House and asked for more and more.

Was it not possible, Van Buren asked in chill exasperation, for the forces of the United States to bring an end to the thing?

The generals explained the situation deftly. It was a difficult terrain. Forts must be built. Roads must be constructed, breakwaters erected, wharfs flung far out into the shallow waters of countless muddy bays, the names of which made no sense to the cultured ear from the Hudson River valley.

He sat in his office in the White House, quite alone, before the smoldering coals in the small grate fire, thinking about generals and war, and about this Seminole affair, that wandered on year after year, reaching no end, never pointing to any conclusion.

"All wars," he thought irritably, "are incomprehensible after thirty years, even the important and socially correct ones." He considered that idea. Certainly, he mused, there were social distinctions in wars as in everything else. This Seminole war had no social attractions. In New York, except in southern trading circles, you scarcely ever heard it mentioned. In his own experience there was nothing more tiring than to discuss, with an old veteran, the campaigns of the Revolution, with their endless mistakes and dissensions. As far as the second British war was concerned, the War of 1812—as some of the historians were beginning to call it—no one ever discussed it at all, except, of course, the westerners and Andrew Jackson.

He considered again his old chief, as he had many times before, in affectionate detail.

"Jackson," he concluded, "loved war. He loved war for the deep thrill of it. To a man who loves war there is no excitement in life that can be compared to fighting a regiment, a division or an army—or a navy too, for that matter. The sense of unleashed power, not only over your own men but the men against you—the men you are going to whip, is elemental. All men who have the gambler's spirit succumb to it. Jackson never quite got over it.

"But Jackson hated it, too," he went on. "He hated

its confusion, its waste and destruction." Van Buren thought of the numberless times he had heard the Old General denounce war.

"War is essentially waste and destruction," he thought. "Not only the destruction that your enemy wreaks on you or that you succeed in bringing about in the course of a campaign. Such waste is frequently the lesser evil. It's the fearful waste caused by your own people, your incompetents, your short-visioned bung-eyed officials, and the sycophantic, demagogic waggle-tails on the hill. They are the great wasters in war."

Was there any remedy?

"If only capable men with large vision could run the wars," he thought. He checked himself. "Large visioned. Well, if they were large visioned and able they would rarely have a war. For it was the business of competent national leaders to foresee the frictional points that make war and by foreseeing them eliminate and forestall war."

Weakness, he felt, was the vital factor. Nations go to war because they dare not stay out. Fears force men into the maelstrom or their very weakness subjects them to attack.

He brooded on Jackson, the Old General.

"He wasn't weak. He had vision. The South Carolina affair, for instance. He foresaw that and he understood its implications. So he took steps. He avoided war. And for the time the people won."

That had been Jackson's big problem. He had had to

bequeath the Seminole question to his successor. There the Seminoles were, slipping away in the black shadows of the Everglades with the generals splashing after them.

The weary years were going drearily by. Generals came and went. Some were lost in the depths of the live oak and palmetto scrub, then came sloshing back through the black waters with a few prisoners and some casualties. It was not, the experts pointed out, the sort of war they had expected. They did not add that no war ever is the sort of war the experts expect. But the flitting Seminoles remained; the hungry cattlemen still eyed the lush ranges of the Florida hinterland with unrelieved desire, the pressure of the outraged southern planters for the extinction of this haven for runaway property persisted, and the war went on.

With the arrival of Colonel Worth at Tampa Bay, a new policy of adjustment and compromise was tried. The Indians, for their part, tired of the years of conflict, came in to talk with this man whom they had learned to trust. By the summer of 1842, with almost twelve thousand Seminoles transported to the plains of Oklahoma, Worth, announcing that there were but four hundred Indians still left in the 'Glades, declared the war was over. A lull set in and for over a decade scarcely a shot was fired in anger along the Florida frontier.

CHAPTER 13

BILLY BOWLEGS' BANANA PATCH

BILLY BOWLEGS' banana patch once set the fires of war alight again along the Mangrove Coast. For fifteen years there had been little Indian trouble along the Gulf. Billy Bowlegs, a stocky, personable Seminole, who had achieved leadership over the scattered remnant of the tribe, kept himself deep in the Big Cypress country. He was seen now and again around Fort Myers and among some of the new settlements on the Manatee and around Sarasota Bay, and seemed to everybody a comic rather than a sinister figure. With a brave or two with him, he would stop at settlers' homes to enjoy a meal. He liked especially to visit the Whitakers' place near the bayou on Sarasota Bay and called in often.

"If you ever fight us again, Billy," said Mary Wyatt Whitaker one day as the Indian hung about the porch after a large dinner, "would you kill me?"

"Oh, yes, kill," said Billy earnestly. "But I do it easy."

But he liked Mary Whitaker, who had married young Bill and had helped make him a home on the rich ham-

158

mock off the bay, and he knew Mary could pick off a turkey with her rifle any morning before breakfast at one hundred yards and never touch feather of its body save the head. He knew she could ride better than most of the men and could equal any Seminole at handling one of the long, tree-trunk canoes the Indians used.

Billy, left to himself, was all for peace. His scattered band numbered not more than four hundred souls, which meant less than a hundred fighting men. Billy was under no illusions about his ability to stand off the whites. His policy was simple. Keep the Seminole camps deep in the 'Glades, try hard to keep the tribesmen out of town, and never let the settlers locate the distant hammocks upon which his people lived.

But the high-topped beaver hats in the Land Office in Washington decided upon a Florida survey. The army was to co-operate. Lieutenant George Hartsoff with a squad of eight armed men and two unarmed teamsters from Fort Myers was ordered into the Big Cypress country in December 1855, to help establish the lines. The little squad worked south and east for two weeks. And then, one ill-starred afternoon, some of the soldiers stumbled on Billy Bowlegs' banana patch. It was more than a banana patch; it was a garden of considerable extent and Billy's choicest possession. The banana plants were over fifteen feet in height and the bananas were the joy of every Seminole papoose. Billy often took clusters of them in to Fort Myers to present to his white friends.

It had been a dull and boring period for the soldiers in the woods and now, the week before Christmas, there seemed small chance of getting back to Fort Myers. No chance, with Hartsoff in command, to do anything but run the survey. And so, as they explained afterwards, "just for hell to see old Billy cut up," the boys tore up the banana patch, broke down the stalks, smashed the pumpkins and made targets of the squash. Then they left.

A few hours later Billy Bowlegs got back to camp. He looked about him. The wreckage burned him up.

Lieutenant Hartsoff's men, clustered round the cook tent, thought it uproariously funny. When Billy demanded compensation in cash for their damage, it was side-splitting. They pushed each other around and howled as Billy made his demands. Then they started pushing Billy. One of them shoved him and another tripped him, and he fell on his flat, round face. The whole camp screeched at that. Billy, saying nothing, faded away. The boys didn't notice where because Hartsoff had turned up with the announcement that they would break camp in the morning and go back to Fort Myers. Was that news! Boy! A cinch they couldn't get back in time for Christmas but they might make New Year's!

The camp slept lightly that night, in a fever for the start.

But over in Billy Bowlegs' camp the Indians were wide

awake. Long after midnight the campfire blazed at the
end of the ruined garden patch. From time to time a new
Indian would arrive. Soon Billy had with him a dozen
fighting men. Runners were sent to call in more. Over and
over Billy recited what had happened. He showed them
the broken garden. He told the story of his maltreatment
by the soldiers. Long before morning the war paint was
smeared on, the plan of attack devised.

Half an hour before daylight, the eight soldiers and the
two teamsters were up. Their cook-fire burned brightly as
they gulped down their coffee. All the tents were down
except Hartsoff's, and the glimmer through its canvas
walls showed that the lieutenant too was up. The little
camp lay between two low hammocks, the one to the
right marked by a grove of pines; the other higher and
closer to the camp was overrun with a tangle of grape
vine, creeper, wild oat and palmetto scrub. The eager
men, walking back and forth between the two hammocks
from the fire to the wagons, were thrown into bright relief against the shadows from the near-by trees. Three of
the men were out of the way some distance off from the
fire with the horses.

Suddenly a wild scream arose from one of the hammocks! A yammering chorus of staccato yells! Then came
the long flashes from a half dozen old muzzle loaders.
Two of the men at the horses' heads jumped to their
beasts and escaped. Four men had been shot down

around the campfire in the first blast. Hartsoff burst out of his tent half dressed, his revolver in his hand, shouting: "For God's sake, what is it?"

The dim figures of the three men against the rear wheels of the farthest wagon were all he sighted. Running low across the circle of ground softly lighted by the dying campfire, shooting as he ran, he managed to join the others. As he swung around the wagon a rifle ball clipped his arm just above the elbow. He scarcely noticed it. The three privates, huddled low behind the off wheel, returned fire to the black shadows fifty yards away. Bullets whistled all about, smashing into the sideboards of the wagons.

"Are you all that's left?" Hartsoff shouted. "Where are all the men? Are they all killed but you?"

The man he was shouting at crumpled up before him without a sound, and fell heavily, rolling on his face. His third man, farthest away, already down on his knees, rolled over and started a slow belly-crawl toward the shadows of the low hammock, dragging his rifle with him as he went. The last man dropped to the ground, taking what protection he could from the heavy spokes of the wheel and the shadows from the wagon box.

"Pull down here," he called to the lieutenant. "Do you want to get banged again?"

Suddenly behind them a rifle started firing into the Indians.

"Bully," shouted Hartsoff.

A second later a rifle ball caught the lieutenant in the chest and threw him back on his side. Blood spurted from the wound and spread over his clothes.

"Get back," whispered the soldier beside him. "There's still two of us to keep them off."

Taking the officer's revolver, he fired one shot. Then he quickly fired his own rifle, trying to conceal the fact of Hartsoff's injury and cover his retreat in the darkness.

It was growing perceptibly lighter. The long, green-gray streak over the eastern horizon was turning amethyst about its edges and diffusing itself into a thin layer of pink against the darker morning sky. The shooting from the Indians' hammock died away. Hartsoff, reaching cover in the palmettoes and grass, fainted. The man behind the wagon wheel worked slowly back toward the hammock. He called softly. There was no response from Hartsoff. The other private joined him and the two, staggering weakly, slid from sight into the marsh grass in the first green light of the morning.

Five days later, a detachment from Fort Myers found Hartsoff delirious, too weak to stand, some fifteen miles from the scene of the attack. Four of his men had escaped to reach Fort Myers. Troops were sent out at once. Hartsoff, coming to, heard an Indian scrambling on the outskirts of the hammock, grunting, "Come out. Come out." He had lain still, too weak to do much else. After hours of hiding, he tried to crawl through the grass, seeking water. When he came to a small pond, he lay on his face, trying to get moisture. His lips had hardly touched the water when an excited hiss and cough warned him and he lifted his face to stare into the mouth of an alligator, drawn to the scene by the scent of blood. For hours he had struggled on and then, exhausted, was compelled to lie still for what seemed to him days on end. Once he thought he lay for thirty-six hours without moving. Only thirst drove him on. He found a piece of paper and, using a stick and blood from his wound, wrote a brief message and pinned it on his coat. He expected the end. A few hours later soldiers came upon him near the ruins of the abandoned stockade called Fort Drum. He lay in the slime of the swamp, the message still pinned to his coat.

Meantime, Billy Bowlegs had struck swiftly north and south. His few warriors he used in fours and sixes to make sudden forays on isolated farmhouses, taverns and small army posts. Three Indians raided Carney's ferry on the Alfaia, just south of Tampa, kidnaped a child and killed a ferryman. Others raided north up the valley of Peace Creek, turning westward to reach the headwaters of the Manatee. Here they found the great house of Dr. Braden on the river banks—Braden's Castle. It was brightly illuminated, for the Doctor, an old Tallahassee man and a former Virginian, was entertaining some important men from Tallahassee, and his old friends, Furman Chaires of the great Chaires plantation and the Reverend T. T. Sealey. A kitchen-maid saw a shadowy form on the back piazza, and screamed. Lights were blown out and shutters slammed. After a brisk volley or two the Indians slipped away, raiding the slave quarters as they went, kidnaping half a dozen Negroes and "three of the doctor's best mules."

Bill Whitaker, husband of Mary, rode four days eastward into the Florida jungle to reach the nearest military force at the headwaters of the Peace; the Braden home, built solidly of "tabby" and cypress, was turned into a refugee fort, three companies of militia under John Lesley of Tampa were organized, and for nine months the families of the Manatee Valley and Sarasota Bay districts lived under the protection of the walls of Braden's Castle. The Whitaker home on Sarasota Bay was raided, and an Irish farm hand, whose contempt for the Indians made him refuse to flee, was found dead in the burning embers of the house. To the north, the country about Fort Meade suffered many raids. The long military road, built from Fort Brooke, at Tampa south through Manatee, along Sarasota Bay, where Captain Davenport had commanded two companies of federal troops, and on to Boca Grande and Fort Myers, was again and again crossed by marauding Indians. But the end was never in doubt. In 1858 Billy Bowlegs, with one hundred and thirty-nine survivors of his tribe, were herded on Egmont Key in lower Tampa Bay, and there put on board transports for the west.

Only Tiger Tail, a young sub-chief, escaped. In the

morning, as the Seminoles were being lined up for embarkation, Tiger Tail asked Sampson, a Negro interpreter, for a glass of water. Pouring a pinch of powdered glass into the water, he drank and spread his blanket upon the beach. Within an hour he was dead.

A hundred Seminoles, it was believed, were still hidden in the Everglades. Too weak to harm anybody, too elusive to catch, the Government was only too willing to forget them.

It is from these hundred seedling Seminoles that today's estimated five or six hundred of the tribe still in Florida derive. Small in numbers as they are, they still fall into the two historic groups that have always divided the Seminole people. The Cow Seminoles, occupying the thirty-seven thousand-acre reservation just south of Brighton, are Muscogees. The Seminoles of the Big Cypress Swamp country, on the reservation in Hendry County, are Micosukees. The Muscogee Seminoles are an agrarian people. They own large numbers of cattle which they herd with an intelligent understanding of modern range management. Their children go to school, and the older Indians often go to night school to learn to read and write. The Muscogees tend to retain their native type of shelter and most of the women still wear the colorful native dress, yet nearly every home on the reservation has both an automobile and a sewing machine. The Muscogee Seminole brave dresses like any Florida cowboy, except on ceremonial occasions.

As the Everglades have been drained and the wild life reduced, the Muscogees have had to look more to their gardens. Their hog pens and cattle have furnished their livelihood.

Deeper in the Big Cypress Swamp the Micosukees hold to the old way of life. They hunt and fish. They use the old dugout canoe and the men still dress in the knee-length shirt. The dialects of the two groups differ so that it is difficult for them to understand each other.

By and large the Federal Government lets them govern themselves. They enforce their own code—even in murder—and they keep their ancient rites for marriage and burial. They hold to their mysteries, which few white men have ever even tried to penetrate. They also kept their ancient, deep resentment against the Government of the United States and all of its works until these last few years. Deep in the Everglades, for a century, tales of the Seminole wars were handed down from father to son and the flame of suspicion and dislike burned steadily. Only in the last twenty years has an effort been made to quench it and find a way to better understanding.

The Seminoles seen along the Tamiami Trail and lurking in the suburbs of the larger Florida resort cities, are ill regarded by the Reservation Seminole, and the Indians' best friends among the whites feel that the roadside exhibition camps create such an artificial life for the Indian that no good can come of these sops to the tourists.

On the reservations the Seminole seems to live a natural and healthy existence. Their numbers increase—their wealth, too—and they have more and more understanding of their white neighbors. They are ideally qualified to take over and operate great sections of the swamp land of Florida which no white men could ever effectively handle. The State and the Federal Government now use tact and care in dealing with the situation. They impose few restrictions on the Indians and take care that the avenues of contact are open, so that when and if the Seminole chooses to enlarge his association with the white man's culture, he may do so to the exact degree he desires.

CHAPTER 14

THE F. F. V.'S GO SOUTH

TALLAHASSEE'S claim to commercial consideration was the fact that the Pensacola-St. Augustine trail bisected the St. Mark's, Florida, to Thomasville, Georgia road. In the years to come thousands of bales of cotton were pulled into St. Mark's via the mule-powered railroad, one of the first in the United States, or by the great six-mule teams that were used to haul the cotton vans to the St. Mark's water-side. Because of this, just prior to the Civil War Tallahassee was one of the best mule markets in the country. They were herded south each fall from Tennessee, South Carolina and Georgia.

By 1821 the absorption of the free lands, the rapid deterioration of the existing cotton areas and the sharp narrowing of the sectors of easy opportunity, brought Florida to the attention of the uneasy minds of dissatisfied men in the older southern states. Florida had a reputation for its climate and as a distant, but attractive, winter resort. These swung to the new territory the best of the last great wave of emigration to the south before the final sweep to the western frontier. Sons and daughters from many of the finest plantation homes of Virginia, the Carolinas, Maryland and Georgia, came to take up land and to re-create in northwestern Florida the plantation system as they had known it in their homes. From the tobacco culture of Virginia they moved to a cotton economy. They brought their slaves, their agricultural implements and methods, their fine furniture of mahogany and rosewood, their silver and glass and the traditions of a gracious though fragile civilization. All was transplanted to their broad and fertile acres in Leon and Jefferson counties by the Waltons, Gadsdens, Chaires, Duvals, Calls, Brevards, Bellamys, Turnbulls, Wirts, Parkhills, Craigs, Nuttals and DuPonts. Many of their names are written across the map of Florida, and all of them had a determining hand in the political and social structure of the state.

Ralph Waldo Emerson thought very little of Tallahassee in 1826. It was, he wrote in his journal, "a grotesque place" settled very largely by "office holders, speculators and desperados." He had met a gentleman from North Carolina during his visit there who entertained him with "some of the monstrous absurdities of the Methodists at their Camp Meetings."

"He related an instance," noted Emerson carefully, "of several of these fanatics jumping about on all fours, imitating the barking of dogs, surrounding a tree, in which they pretended to have 'treed Jesus.'"

The town was tough. Arbitrarily established as the capital, located where it was for no other reason than geographical and political need and the beauty of its site, not economic logic, it was not surprising that it had hardly grown at all in the three years since it was surveyed. The territorial council held its first meeting there in 1824. Communications were the immediate problem of the new territory. A poor trail between Pensacola and St. Augustine had existed in Spanish times, but except in the best of weather, it took weeks to follow. One had to camp on the trail, flooded streams were hard to ford in the rainy season, vast stretches of swamp land had to be waded through, and the mosquitoes and red bugs knew no mercy.

Bad bronchial tubes drove young Ralph Waldo Emerson to St. Augustine in 1826, but it was Prince Achille Murat, nephew of Napoleon and the eldest son of Caroline Bonaparte and Joachim Murat, King of Naples, who lured him to Tallahassee. With the crash of the Napoleonic regime and Joachim Murat's execution, Caroline fled to Vienna. Young Achille followed Joseph Bonaparte to Baltimore where the latter had both successfully and disastrously courted turbulent Betsy Patterson. On a visit to Washington, Murat fell in with General R. K. Call, Florida's delegate to Congress, who interested him in the agricultural land around Tallahassee. Congress had given Lafayette the free grant of an entire township not far from Tallahassee; the town had been selected as the site of the future state's capital. Murat, just under twenty-five, seeing a future, set out for the South and purchased land about sixteen miles from the little town, and there established his first plantation, Econchattie. It was there the young Emerson visited for some weeks the sprig of Napoleonic nobility. Murat was a professing atheist. Emerson's faith in immortality was strong and, as he wrote in his journal, "I trust indestructible." The two youngsters argued long into the night. The year after Emerson's visit, Murat vainly attempted to interest his New England friend in returning to Tallahassee to preach. "Your church is rapidly increasing in Georgia. Why should it not extend to Tallahassee and you come there to substitute reason for learning and morality for nonsense, ignorance and fanaticism? Even those who do not think as you do would be glad of it."

When Murat married Catherine Grey, a young widow, a belle in the local Virginia colony and a grandniece of George Washington, a pretty twist for genealogists was set. By this marriage "Katie" Grey became the grandniece of Napoleon Bonaparte and George Washington, and became the cousin of Napoleon III. He, in his turn, made her a "Princess of France." When the convulsion of the Civil War left her penniless it was he that saw to it that she received an annual pension from his funds of fifty thousand francs a year.

Mr. and Mrs. Murat settled at Lipona, their plantation in Jefferson county, where they were hedged about by the bigger plantations of the Gambles, the George Noble Joneses, the Turnbulls, the Parkhills and the Gadsdens. The Frenchman's interests were never confined to cotton. He experimented with plants brought in from South America, southern Europe and Africa; he enjoyed hunting, took part in the Seminole wars as an officer under General Call and unceasingly engaged in scientific experiments. As he grew older, his interests in the scientific field more and more absorbed him. He changed in his habits, became slovenly in his dress and person—odd in the son of Joachim Murat, greatest of coxcombs. Writing to Mrs. Ellen Long shortly after the Civil War, he swore he would never drink water without first seeing to it that it was well impregnated with brandy, and once when he slipped into a large boiler of warm syrup, his first exclamation was, "My God, Katie will make me wash." He boasted that he never removed his boots until they were worn out and it was only by wiles that William, his valet, ever got him out of his clothes. He was inordinately proud of his abilities as a cook. Once when both his wife and the cook were away and unexpected guests arrived, he ordered his Negroes to clip off the ears and tails of all the pigs in the barnyard and from these materials made a "savory dish."

"It is a pity," he told his guests, "that pigs are not all ears and tails."

He investigated every sort of animal and wild growth as possible sources of food.

"Alligator tail soup," he used to say, "would do nicely, but the buzzard is not so good."

Under the American occupation communications gradually improved, and Tallahassee began to grow. The tides of immigration into the area about Tallahassee continued steadily with noteworthy additions from Missouri, Indiana, Kentucky and the New England states. A mail-stage arrived twice a week. It still took a full three weeks to send a letter from New York to the capital, and it was often easier for a resident of Key West to take passage to New York and thence go by stage to Tallahassee than to wait for a possible passage from Key West to the upper gulf coast. The annual session of the territorial council was the social, commercial and, of course, political climax of the year. There were few commercial establishments and even fewer places of entertainment, yet visitors seemed to like the place. Whisky was sold in every store or inn as a matter of course. Ten cents a gallon was the standard price. It was good corn whisky, clear and unadulterated, and everybody—almost—drank freely of it. Ministers drank it; laborers drank it. All politicians drank it. Most of the ladies took it straight, sipping it delicately with a small glass of water as a chaser.

"Race week," reports Caroline Bravard in her excellent "History of Florida", "was a gala time. Everyone went to the races. The stakes were rather high and gambling general."

"Nothing is talked of here," a young lady wrote home while visiting Tallahassee in the early 'thirties, "except the races and the meetings of the Temperance Society."

An attempt to colonize the Lafayette township with French immigrants was unsuccessful, but a number of French families did settle in the vicinity of Tallahassee and these, with Murat and a few other families from central Europe, gave the town a cosmopolitan atmosphere that it retains to this day. But the dominant families were the big planters whose "places," often running into thousands of acres, were worked by slave colonies that numbered hundreds of persons. The problem of feeding these Negroes became ever more pressing. To raise or obtain cheap slave food was almost as vital in the economics of the plantation as the raising of the cotton crop.

Cotton was a crop that required considerable financing. As the 'thirties wore along it became clear that the problem of communications was not being solved by the dirt roads. Something would have to be done about railroads and canals, new and better sailing packets and improved steamship service. All this required more money than the primitive banking resources of the territory could hope to supply. There had always been a strong anti-bank feeling in Florida, and four attempts to secure bank charters from the territorial council were vetoed over a considerable period of time by Governor Duval. Without banking facilities the planters had been forced to utilize the services of the trading companies, and while these would serve as a source of credit for current plantation requirements, it was obvious they could not meet the needs of any wide plan of internal improvement.

While other interests of the territory organized the Bank of Pensacola and the Southern Life Insurance and Trust Company, the Virginia planters under the leadership of Colonel John G. Gamble promoted the big Union Bank of Tallahassee. It was a three-million-dollar concern frankly copied after the plan of the Bank of Louisiana, its basic capital provided by an issue of State bonds, the interest and principal of which was to be paid by the Bank. Its officers and directors were found among the Gambles, of whom John G. Gamble was its president and Robert Gamble a director, as were Chaires, Nuttals, and others in the prosperous planter group. The Union was definitely a planter's bank. All of the wealthiest of the Virginia planters in Leon and Jefferson counties were involved in its promotion.

Governor Duval, who had been frankly anti-bank, took occasion to urge its creation. The Gambles, between them, took over thirteen hundred shares at one hundred dollars per share. The method of financing was simple. Each subscriber made a small cash payment down with his subscription. For the balance of the sum due he gave a mortgage upon his plantation, slaves or other property presumed to be twice the value of the amount owed upon the shares. With his shares safely in his pocket the planter was then able to borrow two-thirds of the value of his shares from the bank in order to extend and develop his plantation.

It seemed to be a wonderful scheme. During the blooming 'thirties men scrambled to get possession of the Union Bank shares.

"It's the best thing afloat," wrote a young Florida planter to a friend in the Spring of 1838. "A man can almost go to sleep and wake up rich. One or two good crops of cotton will redeem all your obligations at the bank." And one or two good crops of cotton did redeem the obligation as long as cotton was high and the demand from the great mills in the Lancashires and New England pressing.

But the creeping paralysis of commercial stagnation that had begun to grip Europe and New England at last reached Tallahassee. The impact of the Seminole war upon Florida land values was depressing. Yellow fever swept St. Joseph's, in whose boom town properties the Union Bank had invested heavily. St. Joseph's blew up. The State of Florida suddenly found itself confronted with the probability of having to pay both the interest and principal of the "faith" bonds upon which the bank's three-million-dollar capital was based. The grip of the depression tightened; stockholder loans suddenly became bad assets; plantation values crashed; slaves and movable property, pledged in share purchases, disappeared. Men began to whisper; deposit withdrawals started. The inevitable swiftly happened. The Union Bank closed.

In the wreck of the Union Bank was a large portion of John G. Gamble's fortune; almost all of Robert Gamble's liquid assets, and the fortunes of the Bradens, the Chaires and others suffered serious hurt. Many liquidated as best they could and went away; others fought, went back to Virginia and the Carolinas for additional funds, determined to stay in Florida and recoup their fortunes.

That was what the Gambles, the Bradens and the Craigs did. Far to the south, below Fort Brooke on Tampa Bay, they had heard of the fertile hammocks of the Manatee. The Federal Government was just opening the land for settlement.

In 1842, tired with legal disputes, family recriminations, and unpleasant memories associated with the bank's crash, Robert Gamble departed on a land prospecting trip to Manatee. Sugar cane, he believed, could be raised with profit there.

CHAPTER 15

OPENING UP THE MANATEE

IF it was the crash of the Union Bank of Tallahassee that sent the pioneering sons of far-away Virginia scuttling from Leon county to the hammocks of the Manatee in search of rich sugar land and a new future, it was the glowing enthusiasm of Captain Frederick Tresca, skipper of the coastwise trader *Margaret Ann,* drew Josiah Gates to the Manatee to become its first permanent white settler. That was in January, 1842.

Gates was in his forties, a hotel keeper at Fort Brooke and prosperous. Visiting army officers with business at the bustling fort, the chief supply station of the army in the Seminole wars; traveling governmental inspectors; civilians in charge of the Indian removal plans; and, even in that day, a few tourists, had provided Mr. Gates with a sound and profitable custom. But in the language of his times he was "still looking round." Among his regular guests were Captain Tresca, born in Dankert, France, who had been a cabin boy on the frigate *Bellerophon* when it took the pale and drooping Napoleon from

France toward St. Helena, and Captain Archibald Mc-
Neill, an Argyllshire Scot, lured to Tampa Bay by the
prospect of profitable shipping. Near by lived young
Henry Clark, a Canton, New York, merchant seeking a
location. It was Tresca who sold the Manatee to Josiah
Gates, to Archibald McNeill and to Henry Clark, and
Archibald McNeill who taught young James McKay the
mysteries of navigation. McNeill, McKay, and Tresca together established the commercial shipping that has since
grown into the great port of present-day Tampa. The
ships of Archibald McNeill were the first to cruise from
the mouth of the Manatee to New York, Providence and
Baltimore. The schooners which carried the sugar from
the Manatee refineries to warehouses at New Orleans and
Mobile were McNeill's. They kept the stores of Tampa
and Manatee filled with bolts of dress goods, millinery,
high beaver hats, and broadcloth for suits, kitchenware,
pottery and the furniture and gear essential even to pioneering households. McKay's vessels opened the cattle
trade with Cuba, and Tresca's coastwise sloops made life
possible for the isolated bay fishermen and for the Snells,
the Petersons and Atzeroths who later took up land on
the keys and created fine plantations there. The secrets
of all the shallow bays and inside routes from the Manatee to Key West became the stock in trade of the Trescas
—and a matter of importance and historical consequence
later on. In the long and dreary days of the War between
the States the McKays, the McNeills and Trescas ran in

many a cargo of iron and lead and the precious quinine, coffee, and salt that kept Lee facing north until April '65 and Appomattox. And in 1898 it was a McKay who stood on the bridge of the *Gussie*, first American transport under Spanish fire, and landed a Cuban contingent upon that island's shore. But none of this was even dreamed of when Captain Tresca and the *Margaret Ann* unloaded Josiah Gates upon a rising hammock on the south shore of the Manatee and hurried back to Fort Brooke to get Henry Clark and his family, who were to settle on the quarter section directly west of Josiah Gates. By the time they got there, Gates and his eight Negro slaves had already built a six-room cabin, with a passage and a detached kitchen. The Gates House was ready for business. White settlement on the Manatee had begun.

South of the mouth of the Manatee lay the angular length of Longboat Key which frames the western boundary of Sarasota Bay. For over a century itinerant Spanish and Cuban fishermen had maintained a fishing camp and Indian trading station near today's village of Long Beach. The old charts show the camp as Saraxola. As Saraxola on some of the old charts it likewise gave its name to the adjoining body of water, Saraxola Bay. Probably the first European recognition given to the Sarasota Bay region was the publication of the famous La Moyne map of 1591. Tampa Bay is indicated there as Sinus Ioan nis

Ponce and the opening to the south now named Sarasota
Pass was called R. Canotes (Canoe river). Spanish naval
charts of 1768 call Sarasota Bay as Puerto de Saxasote.
With the British occupation of Florida the chart makers
began referring to Sarazota Bay. By 1840 American us-
age had slurred the Sarazota into Sarasota. By 1850 Sarasota was the accepted spelling on all maps.

But it was for Saraxola that William Whitaker, in 1843
out of St. Marks, Florida, with a party of fisherman
friends looking for land, steered his small schooner. They
found a lonely Spaniard, Elzwarthy, at the abandoned
camp. It was he who advised Whitaker to take up land
on a likely hammock to the east across the bay. Whitaker's
warrant entitled him to one hundred ninety-nine acres,
and in partnership with his brother-in-law, Simon
Snell, the hammock was staked out and the settlement
which developed into the city of Sarasota was begun. It
was Simon Snell who first imported Cuban guavas into
west Florida and began their cultivation.

For centuries the sheltering keys along the gulf coast
had entertained itinerant Spanish fishermen. Working
north from Cuba in search of the great schools of mullet
and kingfish, these men of dubious reputation established shacks upon the keys extending from the mouth of
the Shark to Tampa Bay. James Grant Forbes, who
visited west Florida in 1772, spoke of the keys to the
south of Tampa Bay as being the "haunt of the picaroons

of all nations." John Lee Williams in his very rare and valuable book "The Territory of Florida" written in 1833, records that the noted British Seminole traders, Ambrister and Arbuthonut, who were hung in 1818 by Andrew Jackson, had an extensive plantation south and east of the mouth of the Manatee. This must have been about 1815. Over two hundred slaves were employed on the place, which, according to Williams, was abandoned after the death of the owners.

Optimistic New York real estate speculators had a finger on the keys as early as 1833. One group built "an elegant house" and several smaller homes on the southeastern side of Sanibel Key in Charlotte Harbor. The boom failed to develop and by 1837 the houses had begun to decay. A number of plantations on the Charlotte Harbor keys owned by Cubans and a solitary American, named Dixon, were said to be growing papayas, oranges, and vegetables with success a hundred years ago.

Away from the rivers the settlement along the Mangrove Coast south of Fort Brooke developed slowly. Twenty-five years had passed since the United States government had taken possession of Florida and Florida was three years old as a state when Congress in 1846 finally authorized an appropriation to erect a lighthouse on Egmont Key in lower Tampa Bay. In the sultry darkness of the tropical nights its light was the only gleam between Key West and St. Marks. Destroyed in the hurricane of 1848 it was immediately rebuilt. The light on Egmont Key still welcomes the swelling sea-borne traffic in and out of Tampa Bay.

Profits out of the sugar trade were mounting; the price of land was going up. Henry Clark was dead, but at the old Clark store on the Manatee calico was selling for twelve and a half cents a yard; a pair of kid gloves cost a dollar eighty and broadcloth was selling for four and a half dollars per yard. Good brandy was seventy-five cents a bottle and six linen shirts cost two and a half dollars each. Merchandise was far from cheap but business was brisk. Sugar was a good cash crop and the fertility of the land was beyond belief. Some of the ladies were reading "Godey's Lady's Book" and importing silk lace half-mitts and a current novelty in costume jewelry made of human hair—chic. Any lady who wished to have her spare locks made into a bracelet could be accommodated if she would send on the hair and a check for four and a half dollars. In the fall of 1853 the first sewing machine arrived—a Sloat—and it embellished the sewing room of Mrs. Josiah Gates at the big new twenty-room Gates House, just completed with real plaster walls, the finest hotel south of Jacksonville.

CHAPTER 16

THE SUGAR KETTLES

SOME of the best blood of Virginia was in the Gambles and the Bradens. Gamble Hill in Richmond and Gamble Hundred still keep alive the traditions of a family which was a driving force long before Richmond became a capital city. John Gratton Gamble had served with John Marshall when the future Chief Justice was envoy to France, fighting long and hard against the insatiable demands of Talleyrand for American subsidies to support French arms against the British. When Marshall made his final and convincing report of our refusal to pour forth our treasure—we were more respectful of money in those days and a great deal more fearful of European entanglements—John Gratton Gamble followed his chief back to the United States. In Virginia he lived the life of an important planter, married Nancy Greenup, daughter of the Governor of Kentucky, promoted a canal or two on the side, and made contacts with British financial institutions exploring the lost colony. In Virginia his son, young Bob, named for his uncle, was born. It was not until 1827 that John Gratton Gamble and his brother moved to Leon County, Florida, hoping to set up on a cotton foundation the old ample life they had led in Virginia. It was the promotion and crash of the Union Bank fifteen years later that sent Major Gamble and Doctor Joe Braden in midsummer 1842 to the Gates House on the Manatee. The way out and onward, this time, was to be Sugar.

Opening up new hammock land was an old story to both men. Dr. Joe and his brother Hector took up by claim and purchase over a thousand acres south of the Manatee and built their first log cabin on the rising bluff that today is the site of Bradenton. The greater part of their holdings, though, were on the banks of Braden Creek a mile to the east. Major Gamble's choice was for the long fertile level tracts north of the river where it curves to the north and east, and he began to set in order an estate of three thousand acres.

The first families of Virginia were setting up as first families of Florida. Pinckney Craig and his brother John William moved onto a big tract just west and south of the Gambles; and along with them arrived the Wyatts, the Wares, the Ledwiths, the Reeds, and the Snells from Tallahassee, all refugees from the wreck of the Union Bank. In less than a year all of the land south of the Manatee was taken up, and settlers were moving in west of the Gambles and the Craigs in a stream. Major Robert Gamble brought with him a hundred slaves and a ship load of agricultural tools. Sugar refining machinery began to be unloaded in cargoes from New Orleans. The Bradens had over eighty slaves, and the Craigs, too, had brought their colored "people" with them. In less than two years the cane was standing high upon thousands of acres; smoke was pouring out of the chimneys of the sugar mills; the great six-hundred-gallon caldrons were bubbling; and Archibald McNeill's new big schooner, the *Eliza Fiske,* sailed up the Manatee and warped into the Gamble dock to carry its first cargo of sugar and molasses to New Orleans. Other schooners, and even a few sloops nosed in for their share of the trade. Manatee Valley sugar became a factor in the nation's output. High water along the Mississippi year after year in succession flooded the Louisiana cane fields. The demand for the Manatee product was steady. Most of it was distributed through the New Orleans market. By 1845 a dozen large sugar cane plantations were flourishing. Josiah Gates was raising cane as well as conducting the Gates House, and Braden production called for a series of mills of their own along Sugar House Creek. The Craigs were building their own refinery, the huge fifty-foot chimney of which still stands. Eleven feet square at its base, built of locally quarried travertine and home-burned red brick, with its foundation walls over four feet thick, it has resisted wind and rain, hurricane and fire, and the explosive assaults of several raids by northern landing parties from blockading vessels during the Civil War. Simon Turman and

John Jackson, later to leave their imprint upon the growing village of Tampa, arrived from the Middle West. They had come down the Mississippi and chartered a schooner at New Orleans to bring them over. Ezekiel Glazier of Massachusetts came with them and it was Glazier who constructed the big Braden mill. North of the Manatee Bob Gamble was building one of the largest sugar mills in the South. The three big brick buildings, whose foundations still exist, were over three hundred and forty feet in the aggregate. His fields were drained with miles of ditches. Four cisterns were built at the Gamble mills, holding over twenty thousand gallons each. Gamble devised a wooden pipe and with this conveyed the water to the cooking rooms where the huge kettles held the boiling juice. Groups of Negroes armed with long-handled dippers constantly stirred the steaming liquid until each kettle had boiled down to about fifty gallons. The residue was then poured into shallow vats with porous bottoms through which the molasses filtered and the sugar cooled.

In the cane fields gangs of Negro slaves toiled steadily —and at times musically—at the job of ditching, planting and cutting the crop from the three thousand acres of the richest cane land in America. The big mule-drawn wagon loads of cane stalk were brought up to the platforms of the crushing house in which the finest machinery obtainable in America had been installed by the Major. The great grinding rolls of the macerators voraciously awaited the loads of cane that were lifted from the wagons by a crane operated by the largest steam engine in the state—a fifty-horse-power outfit built especially for the job. At the peak of the Gamble operations more than three hundred slaves were employed in the fields and the mills.

By 1850 the Manatee sugar area was in full production. For a decade longer the wide fields of cane were planted and chopped, the great fires in the mills, fed by the fat pine from the near-by forests, so rich in rosin that it fairly dripped from each split log, belched dark clouds of smoke over the river. Every year the sugar fleet sailed up the river, took on its loads from the bowed backs of long, dark lines of chanting field-hands and raced away to be first to New Orleans with the product of the Manatee.

The sugar planters swelled with prosperity. Major Gamble and Dr. Joe Braden began building big houses. The Gamble place and the Braden house became centers of the whole social and commercial life of the Manatee area. And the subsequent history of the region never loses sight of them. Shipyards were opened along the river. The sloop *Leg o' Mutton* brought the mail down from Tampa once a week. Billy Bowlegs' revolt, the last futile outbreak of the Seminoles, was beaten off. As the high-tempered and menacing 'fifties began to fade, the pinch of the Buchanan depression came on. For the second time in his expanding career, the banks began calling on Bob Gamble and again he could not meet his notes.

The Gamble estate, esteemed the best equipped sugar plantation in the country, was sold in 1859 to Cofield and Davis of New Orleans for one hundred and ninety thousand dollars, and Major Bob went back to Leon County.

History moves fast and faster. Sumter and the Secession, the Union Blockade and the late afternoon in 1861 when landing parties from the U. S. blockade schooner *Stonewall* marched up the country roads, destroyed the grist mills on their way, and arrived at the Gamble refineries. Erroneous reports had reached Commodore Theodore P. Green of the Gulf Blockading Squadron that the refineries were owned by Jefferson Davis, and they were regarded as a special prize. Sources of Confederate sugar and molasses they certainly were. So they burned the mills, though they left the mansion and lesser houses of the estate alone, after looting the place of its livestock and utensils. Bombs were placed in the great kettles, and among the heavy rollers, and underneath the fifty-horsepower steam engine that was Major Gamble's pride. Before the sun had set nothing but heavy clouds of smoke slowly drifting toward the waters of the gulf remained of the days of sugar. Cane never revived along the Manatee.

Reverend Ezekiel Glazier and young Bill Whitaker late one afternoon in June, 1865, drove a light spring-wagon piled high with green pine boughs down the trail from Manatee. Against the green of the pines gleamed a hastily scrawled "Fresh Meat for Sale." The wagon clattered down the trail to the mouth of Hog Creek. Here the wagon stopped abruptly, the pine boughs heaved and tossed, and Judah P. Benjamin, Secretary of State for the late Confederate Government, scrambled down upon the solid white sand of the beach on Sarasota Bay.

Eleven weeks before, Benjamin, with President Jefferson Davis and his Cabinet, had dashed out of Richmond for Danville and the south. Benjamin, convinced that the size of the party made escape impossible, left the Confederate President near Washington, Georgia, on May 2nd. Behind a heavy pair of goggles and a straggly beard, Benjamin, calling himself Monsieur Bonfal, a wandering Frenchman interested in the effect of war upon the South, worked his way down through Georgia. Near the Florida line he fell in with Colonel John T. Taylor, who told him of Davis' arrest.

"Will you ever get away with the accent?" Taylor wanted to know. "There is forty thousand dollars on your head, and the Federals are on to every suspicious stranger."

"You forget I'm from Louisiana," said Benjamin. "If they catch me I can speak with a better accent than any Frenchman."

All the same, as Benjamin plunged farther south into Florida, Monsieur Bonfal was abandoned and Farmer Howard emerged. As Farmer Howard, Benjamin reached Brooksville where friends vouched for him to Major John T. Leasley. Leasley confided in James McKay. The two brought Benjamin to Tampa. The little town was swarming with Federal soldiers and sailors and Benjamin was stored in the McKay attic for days. One squall-wracked night his new friends took him south to Major Turner's plantation near Parrish, and thence to the Gamble mansion at Ellenton on the north bank of Manatee. The Gamble house, then as now, was the glamour "place" of the Manatee. Built by Major Robert Gamble in the 'forties it was an exact duplicate of "Waukeenah," the Gamble homestead near Tallahassee, except that the mansion was constructed of great slabs of "tabby" instead of the home-burned red brick of northwest Florida. "Tabby" is a combination of marl, burnt shell lime, oyster shell and sand. Early pioneers along the Georgia coast found that, molded into large slabs and sun dried, it made exceedingly strong walls highly resistant to wind and rain. The slabs have a tendency to fuse together with the years, creating something as solid as if carved from living rock. The walls of the Gamble mansion were over two and a half feet thick. Eighteen large columns reached from the ground to the wide overhang of the roof, supporting the second-story galleries that ran about the entire building. For over a fortnight the distinguished ex-Confederate official hid in the Gamble mansion. Afternoons he studied the river through a long spy-glass from the small upper gallery. Then one day a squad of Federal soldiers surprised him. Luck alone got him and Mr. Archibald McNeill away to the jungle back of the house. Meantime, Captain Frederick Tresca, the one-time skipper of the *Margaret Ann,* had been besought for a boat to escape in to Nassau. Federal soldiers and sailors had destroyed almost all the craft on the Mangrove Coast, but Tresca two weeks later got wind of a sixteen-foot yawl near Clearwater, bought it with Benjamin's money, signed on H. A. McLeod as a general hand and was off Hog Creek in Sarasota Bay waiting for the passenger. Three weeks later the fugitive was in Nassau. Slipping down the coast to Charlotte Harbor the little craft had been once waylaid by a Federal blockade boat, and Benjamin, in a cook's cap and apron, stirring about the sand-box forward with its bed of glowing charcoal embers, had to shiver. His face was daubed with grease and soot, but one of the Yankee sailors had his own idea.

"I don't know who he is," he said, "but I'm damned if ever I saw a Jew cook working on a fishing boat till now." Tresca, who knew the secrets of the inside passage at Knights Key, took the small boat through himself. At the Key he secured a bigger boat, the *Blonde,* and took her into Bimini in safety. The adventurous Benjamin reached Nassau, then on to Havana and London, where he became the legal adviser of Queen Victoria. He paid Tresca fifteen hundred dollars in gold coin, gave him the *Blonde,* and sent ten-yard lengths of black silk to the ladies of the families who had befriended him in the valley of the Manatee. His cavalry saber he gave to James McKay. In a special case above the fireplace in the dining room of the Gamble mansion, the saber hangs today.

One Spring morning in Sarasota in 1886, Colonel J. Hamilton Gillespie carefully teed up his ball, let fly his driver and watched the white dot slowly sink to the turf against the bright green of the scrub palmetto off the fairway.

Golf enthusiasts in Florida like to tell you that this was the first golf ball ever put in play in America. Maybe! Others make the same claim, and the debate grows acrimonious at times. The facts seem to be simple enough. Colonel Gillespie was the general manager of the Florida Mortgage and Investment Company, a Scotch-British group which included the Archbishop of Canterbury among its stockholders. The group had purchased sixty thousand acres near Sarasota from the Disston interests. Late in 1885 some fifty Scotch and English families from the Paisley, Stirling and Hamilton districts arrived in Sarasota. Each had purchased an acreage plot outside the city, and most of them had titles to other lots within the village. Few knew anything at all about farming and none understood any of the special problems presented by the land in Florida. As an experiment in colonization along the Mangrove Coast, it soon took its place with all the others from Juan Ponce de Leon down. Colonel Gillespie, general manager for the company, had other interests however. His job was to manage the company's affairs, but beyond that it was the Colonel's chief intention to have a fly at golf.

He located a natural clearing on the edge of the town, room for a four-hole course. It was on this course, in the bright sunlight in 1886, that Colonel Gillespie took his initial drive. Later the course was enlarged to nine holes and was used as a golf course by the Colonel and his friends for almost twenty years. Alec Browning, one of the last of the original colony, tells of crossing the cleared ground when he was a boy and seeing the Colonel chopping away at the little ball. Although a Scotch lad from Paisley, Browning had never seen a golf game before. He turned to look at the tall, eager Scot, so busily engaged with his little white ball and long crooked club, and he lingered a bit to enjoy the sight.

"Do you play?" asked the Colonel of the boy who confusedly said "no."

"Mon, y'er missing half y'er life," he said.

This, said old Alec, was in May, 1886.

It was Gillespie, it is said, who sold Henry B. Plant on the value of golf as a Florida tourist attraction. Plant hired him to build golf courses for him at Winter Haven, Tampa, Belleair and Havana, Cuba.

When he died on September 7, 1923 while walking across the little course which he had laid out himself and which he loved so well, Gillespie had left his mark on the whole of the Mangrove Coast.

Almost any sunny afternoon, the old yawl is tied up to some fishing dock along the Mangrove Coast. Skipper Hamlin likes best the long municipal dock at Sarasota, but you can find the *Phantom* anchored off the docks at Nokomis-Venice or Cortez just about as often as you'll find it in Sarasota Bay.

Nothing particularly distinguishes the *Phantom*. Built a trifle on the heavy side compared with modern yachts, she can sail in most regattas and excite no special comment.

Yet the *Phantom* is sixty years old at least, the last of the fleet of coastwise trading vessels upon which life once depended all along the Mangrove Coast from the founding of Fort Brooke in 1823 until the railroads pushed south of Tampa round 1900. For almost eighty years the little schooners, sloops and yawls of the Mangrove Coast had things their own way and were the people's only transport.

For years Captain Frederick Tresca's little schooner, the *Margaret Ann*, carried the mail for the people along the Manatee and Sarasota Bay. The *Leg o' Mutton* followed the *Margaret Ann* in the postal service, carrying the mail to Manatee for years. Then steamboats came in after the Civil War and took the lucrative mail contracts away from the smaller sailing vessels and the *Erie*, the *Mary Disston* and the *Rambler* ran the route between Sarasota, the Manatee, and Tampa. Other vessels went north to Cedar Keys to connect with the railroad, and others sailed from Tampa for Charlotte Harbor points and Key West.

The Key West trade always excited the attention of the masters of the light-draft sailing vessels along the coast, and for a long time it was a steady and profitable run. Key West was dependent upon the mainland farmers for most of its vegetables, fresh meat and forage, and the prices fetched were high.

The Sarasota schooner *Vision* was one of the early boats in the trade. She was a fast bit of marine architecture, and Jim Mason, her skipper, counted on two round trips a month. He would leave Sarasota loaded with sweet potatoes below decks, razor-back hogs and chickens above, and averaged a profit of sixty dollars per trip for himself above all expenses. In the 'eighties along the Mangrove Coast that was handsome money.

Mason used to buy sweet potatoes in Sarasota at forty cents a bushel and sell them on the dock at Key West at two dollars and forty cents. Razor-back hogs on the boat cost about four and a half cents a pound and Key Westers were glad to pay nine cents a pound for the same. Later on the *Ruby*, the *Emma*, the *Wild Goose* and the *Rosa* went into the trade. Some went into competition with the *Vision* for the Key West business. Others merely traded at minor points along the coast. Among these boats was the *Emma M. Little*. The *Emma M. Little* is now the old *Phantom*, still sound of hull and mast. Forty years ago she was equipped with a gasoline marine engine. The engine was built so long ago that it does not even carry a serial number and must therefore be one of the oldest marine engines in use in the world today. But in a fog or a dead calm Skipper Hamlin claims it can still kick the old *Phantom* along.

CHAPTER 17

BECKONING PORTS

TAMPA, the town, evolved slowly from the Fort. During the Seminole wars, the white civilians living round Fort Brooke asked for permission to erect their cabins inside the stockade to save them from sudden Indian assaults, and this concentration inside the military reservation halted the building of dwellings in the village area. Levi Collar was one of the first to move his family away from his homestead on the eastern shore of Tampa Bay and put up a cabin under military protection. Collar, who had had a cabin on the Withlacoochee River, was the first white man to study the advantages of the high hammock lying east of the mouth of the Hillsborough River. Drifting into the Tampa Bay country in the summer of 1822, he noted at once the possibilities of the location between river and bay, with a deep channel cutting through white sand right up to the steep banks of the hammock. He marked the fertile spot in his memory as the homesite he wanted for his own, and when he came back the following summer he was bitterly disappointed

to find Colonel George M. Brooke and Lieutenant Gadsden on the spot with a contingent of U. S. troops from
Pensacola. He settled six miles east, and reconciled
himself to selling garden truck to the troops who were
at work building Fort Brooke. When the Seminole wars
broke out and the Commandant wanted to utilize Collar's
knowledge of the country he was invited to bring his
family into the Fort.

One of the old charts of the Fort, dated January 1838,
shows where the officers' homes were situated. Major
Frazer, Lieutenant McCrab and Captain Evans had
homes east of the point dividing the river from the bay.
Next to them was the prisoners' pen, and behind are
shown long lines of marquees where the soldiers must
have been quartered temporarily while "the Long Shed"
and the barracks were in course of construction. The
maps show the tents of "the German Dragoons," with a
large horse shelter close by, and across a narrow roadway,
a small graveyard. Facing the marshy mangrove key,
now called Davis Island, on the tip of the point, was
Frazer's redoubt, flanked by a small park of artillery.
The whole picture is in the map, the two small piers for
rowboats and canoes; the larger and more substantial
wharf leading to the quartermaster's warehouses and Al-
len's store, behind the redoubt up the Hillsborough
River. At the time Fort Brooke was the main supply base
for the soldiers fighting the Seminoles and took care of
upward of three thousand men.

As the Indians fell back into the 'Glades, ploughing and sowing was resumed around the bay, and a colony of Cuban fishermen collected along Spanishtown Creek. A few settlers dared to erect their cabins well beyond the pale of the reservation, and by '31 there were people enough to justify the Post Office to erect a station. Tampa Bay Post Office, it was called, soon clipped to Tampa Bay. In 1834, the state created Hillsborough county, a vast stretch of land later cut up to form ten counties. It was not until 1846 that the ferry began to operate and a non-military store was opened. About that time Simon Turman and John Jackson came up from Manatee. Simon Turman became a probate judge and editor of the weekly "Peninsular." John Jackson surveyed the townsite and named most of the streets north of the fort after the presidents, and when he ran out of presidents, honored Lafayette and Franklin. Looking back over old files, the mileposts of the town's history appear. The year the "streets" got their name, the county commissioners ordered the construction of a "road" between Bell's Ford on the Alafia River nine miles south of Tampa to Turman's Landing on the Manatee. It couldn't be more than a blazed trail from one creek ford to another, but it gave the early cattlemen a chance to drive their animals south to the ranges, and it offered a path for an occasional horseman to get safely through the bush to Tampa Bay. Years later, even, the record is that it took five days to drive from Manatee to Tampa Bay, a distance of forty miles.

The beginnings of Tampa were no better than might have been expected. Along with the soldiers who packed the Fort and the sailors who made port with the big fleet of supply schooners constantly anchored in the river, came a horde of camp followers out for profits.

"To say that our city was infested with gamblers, No. 1 blacklegs, burglars, thieves, robbers and cutthroats of every shade and high and low degree," said the "Peninsular," afterward discussing the founding of Tampa, "is but speaking the simple truth. One morning a man, a noted villain, was found swinging to a pine tree. A few were whipped. Others were warned and got their orders to leave. The effect was electrical. Robberies ceased. Gamblers fled."

The sweep wasn't as clean as all that. Plenty of color and trouble remained in the struggling little village. Postmaster De Launay's passionate pen set down for the editorial page of the "Peninsular" his protests against the irregularity and the dishonesty with which the United States Mails were handled. For all his precautions, money was stolen from nearly every sack.

The advertising in editor Turman's paper gives another chapter away. The Georgia lotteries were the "Peninsular's" best advertisers. The Georgia State Lottery and the big Consolidated Lottery of Macon paid out for seductive half-pages. The Georgia State in the Spring of 1860 operated an attractive sweep, with a capital prize of sixty thousand dollars, in the interests of the Monticello Academy. Full tickets were priced at ten dollars each, and the drawings were held weekly at Savannah.

"More than one prize to every two tickets," advertised the Georgia State. The old advertisements show how the speculative spirit was early injected into Tampa blood. The ads make good reading—there was the Consolidated of Macon offering three plans of investment, the City, the Havana, and the Combination. The City Plan hung up a capital prize of fifty thousand dollars with tickets at a dollar each; the Havana tempted with a capital prize of seventy thousand dollars; and the Combination held out a one hundred thousand dollar plum. A Combination ticket cost sixteen dollars, and threaded through these offers of so much for so very little were calls for labor. Help Wanted—Agents for the sale of tickets, with juicy commissions hinted. Bank Night at the movies, and the clatter of nickels out of the machine, are nothing to the old days.

The opening of the first cross-state railroad in 1860 quickened the tempo of men and mails, and brought Tampa regularly within a week's journey to New York. Trains left Fernandina on the east coast daily, except Sunday, for Cedar Keys, there to connect with steamers sailing for Manatee and Tampa. True it was quite a while before the railroad really got to the west shore. It ended four miles inland in the bush, and horse carts and wagons got their bit from passengers and baggage dumped at the railhead. Water-borne transport remained the real master of transport for another quarter of a century. The big thousand-ton steamers, the *Galveston* and the *Matagorda*, tapped Tampa twice a month between Texas ports, Key West, Havana and the North. Snappy brigs and sweet-lined schooners sailed out of Tampa monthly in the coastwise trade, and every sort of sail and steamer competed for the passengers and cargo that went south to Havana, or north along the eastern seaboard. History is in the changing cargoes. Texas began to ship ponies to the cowmen of the Florida ranges, and Florida cattle began to move to Cuba. A whole book could be written about the Florida cattle trade. The revival of the cattle business was the first sign of life on the Florida coast after the Civil War.

There were four lawyers in Tampa in 1860, not so much practicing as adventuring in the mazes of the law, and it was one of these that threw off the stiff inhibitions of the profession in the cause of chivalry and pleaded eloquently with the judge for the first and only proxy marriage in the state's florid history. The lady in the case was a widow, and the man in the lumber business "back of Ocala" superintending a cutting job. It would take ten days to get a message to the lady's betrothed and get him back in person to Tampa. His client, said the pleading attorney, "poured out her love like the rush of a river," and the situation was most definitely in the

nature of emergencies. The Judge could but act at once.
The license was fetched and he read the marriage lines
to the lady and her lawyer. Then he mopped his head
and made the single stipulation.

"You tell the groom," he said, "when he gets back here
in Tampa he's not to say anything or see anybody until
he's come up here to me."

Certainly in the spring of that year Tampa, somewhat
out at the elbows, was a rough and tousled conglomera-
tion of cabins, made of log or home-sawn slab, palm-
frond lean-to's and battered tents clustering about the
entrance to the Fort—the youngest, toughest army town
along the nation's southern frontier.

Tampa barracks had spawned a husky garrison brat
that easily took to the wars. The long drawn out conflict
with the Seminoles gave the settlement a strength of
its own, developed out of experience in fighting. The
Mexican War cut the military importance of Fort Brooke
down just when it was best for Tampa to be separated
from military domination. The Civil War did almost no
damage to its men and arms but ruined the economy
that it was defending. A few harmless cannonballs
screamed overhead and landed in the palmetto scrub
and a single cannonball buried itself in Thomas Duke's
kitchen, but looking back on the relations between the
little Confederate garrison in Fort Brooke and the Union
blockading squadron that closely invested the bay and

town almost from the outbreak of the war, the whole affair is amusing, like an old crinoline skirt. The savage effectiveness and brutality of modern war are missing.

True, in April 1863, Lieutenant-Commander William B. Eaton of the U. S. schooner *Beauregard* sent a sharp note to Major R. B. Thomas, commander of the Tampa forces, demanding the immediate evacuation of all women and children and the surrender of the town, threatening to turn loose his cannon. The *Beauregard* was patrolling the waterfront from an anchorage just out of range of the fort's cannon. Major Thomas replied with politeness rejecting the demand for surrender but accepting the suggestion that the women and children be removed.

"I regret that my design of commencing an attack upon Tampa did not meet with your approval," wrote Commander Eaton to the Confederate Major some days later, "but would say in justification of course that the threat to bombard the town was an inadvertence and should have read 'fort' or 'battery' which, however, laid directly in front of and afforded protection to the town. I have the best information from parties who have been in the town but a short time before and made their escape, that the women and children had all been removed from the town and that most if not all the property owners were strong secessionists. You will, I have no doubt, overlook the error in judgment which I have made on taking into consideration the fact that I have been here with my vessel six months and after a long period of inaction I was naturally anxious to give my officers and men another opportunity to show their mettle and afford them the chance they so much desired of doing something if ever so little, toward crippling the enemy. Very respectfully, W. B. Eaton, Lieutenant Commander."

By '63 it was plain that Tampa and the Mangrove Coast must function in the conflict as supply base for the armies of the Confederacy in Georgia and Tennessee. James McKay, Archibald McNeill, and Jake Summerlin were engaged by the Confederacy to secure huge quantities of supplies. The records show that in 1861 Jake Summerlin was marketing over eight thousand head of cattle annually and was Florida's leading cattleman. During the war he drove thousands of Florida steers to Baldwin, the northern railhead, and for the greater part of them, he received no tangible recompense. Archibald McNeill, Frederick Tresca and Donald McKay were blockade running and the *Beauregard*, the *Stonewall* and the *Gem of the Sea*, the barks, *Kingfisher* and *Pursuit* and the tender, *Rosalie*, beating between Charlotte Harbor and Clearwater, were the team that opposed them as they tried to slip through and past bringing up their cargoes from Nassau and Havana. When Sherman marched from Atlanta to the sea and the lower South was definitely cut off from the armies in Virginia, Summerlin and Donald McKay worked in partnership so well, that the blockading Union squadron was in a ferment to the end. Havana, cut off from its normal supply of Florida beef, was in desperate need of meat. Summerlin had cattle. McKay had the *Scottish Chief,* a fast and snappy steam sidewheeler. He had the ship, and he had the map of the channel amid the keys between Charlotte Harbor and the Florida Straits in his brain and marrow. No Federal skipper could match him. The Confederate pair bet their cattle, boat and savvy of the waters against the Union blockade, and pulled off six successful trips to Havana before Appomattox. An eight-dollar Florida steer fetched two sparkling Spanish doubloons on the docks at Havana, and a gold doubloon was worth fifteen sound Union dollars in those days. Flour, sugar, processed tobacco, quinine pills, calico, shoes, suiting and woolen cloth, salt and tea were almost beyond price, they were so scarce. Women's dresses were to be had for five hundred dollars down along the coast, and calico, what there was of it, was parted with for ten dollars the yard. Flour was selling at a hundred and twenty-five dollars a barrel. A Florida ranchman had to turn in fifteen steers to get a barrel of flour, and at that he thought that luck was with him if he found a trader to deal on that basis. Many a Florida ranchman trekked over a hundred miles through nearly trackless jungle to get a box or two of quinine pills, a sack of "real" tobacco and perhaps a pair of shoes. The prices were high, high beyond all reason, but the risks of the blockade runners were tremendous, and McKay and Summerlin knew how to take them. Other runners were caught on their first dash by the Union watchers. Not Captain Frederick Tresca, though, who knew the secret waters of the inner passage as well as McKay, and he made his trips to Nassau until close to the end of the war. Captain John Curry goes down in history, too, as one of the best of the Manatee skippers, but he lost two of his vessels in "the trade." One of them, the *Ariel*, reconditioned by the Yankees, was put to work again in the same waters by the Florida Blockade Patrol.

With the collapse of the Confederacy, cattlemen along the Mangrove Coast stuck together to hold the Cuban trade. Summerlin built a loading station and an eight-hundred-foot wharf at Punta Rassa on Charlotte Harbor. McKay built another on Tampa Bay, and a third was built at Boca Grande. Blazed trails were cut through the jungle and palmetto scrub as far back as the headwaters of the Peace, Miakka and the Manatee, so that the herds could be driven through quickly with the least loss of time and weight. Zibe King, the Carletons, the Hendrys, and the Parkers all became great names in the cattle trade. Dr. H. T. Lykes and his seven sons, founders of the international cattle and shipping firm whose flag is known in ports all over the world, began to play their part. The war was over. New foundations had to be built. The new Florida was founded on beef and doubloons. Many people remember how the cattlemen home from Havana lugged the bulging sacks of gold coin off the boats, threw the clinking bags over their saddle-horns and as carelessly threw them on the floors of the ranch houses until such time as the money was wanted. There were no banks south of Tallahassee until 1883 when Ambler, Marvin and Stockton of Jacksonville, with Senator James Taliaferro, sent young T. C. Taliaferro to Tampa to open the First National. Two gold doubloons sealed in a tin can contrived the standard baby rattle on the big ranches around the headwaters of the Miakka and the Peace.

The somnolent 'seventies passed gently over the Mangrove Coast. A banking panic in Wall Street and a political scandal in Washington could not greatly touch the people who had used Confederate currency for almost two years after Appomattox because they had no other paper currency to use. Spanish doubloons and a few Mexican and Yankee silver dollars were in circulation, but that was all. Doubloons were worth fifteen dollars United States currency, and the hard-bitten people along the Coast needed a money symbol for amounts much smaller than fifteen dollars.

In search of health Sidney Lanier arrived in Tampa in December 1876.

"Tampa is the most forlorn little collection of one-story houses imaginable," he wrote Gibson Peacock in

Philadelphia. But Lanier put up at the Orange Hotel and it was not long before he was entertaining the cream of Tampa's social crop with flute solos.

In 1884 Henry B. Plant and his railroad arrived. The plans for the fantastic Tampa Bay Hotel, now the principal building of Tampa University, were drawn. V. Martinez Ybor with Ignacio Haya, cigar tycoons of Cuba and Key West, seeking a location further away from the internal turmoil of Cuba, came to Tampa. It had been their first thought to bring the factories to the Manatee, but repulsed there, they returned to Tampa. Sanchez and Hayo joined them to bring Ybor City into being and with it the Tampa cigar. Pioneer Tampa was passing. Its population in 1880 was but slightly over eight hundred but by 1885 it had swollen to thirty-five hundred. Even the dreaded yellowjack, which swept in from the West Indies in the summer of 1887, could not hold back the development of the city. Dr. John T. Wall, a leading medical authority of the Tampa district, aroused considerable medical outcry that year when he asserted that he was convinced from his own researches that Dr. Carlos Finlay of Havana had been right when he stated some years previously that the mosquito was the carrier of the disease. Walter Reed's conclusive tests finally fixed the guilt upon the *Stegomyia fasciata* over a decade later, but Dr. Wall's pronouncement and the date of it are remembered in Tampa.

Many distant and divergent things have affected the development of Tampa. California and the gold rush; the Civil War; the bigoted stupidities of the Reconstruction Era, the irresistible pull to the West in the wake of the railroads set the town back. The tempo of its beginning slackened. Decades passed. The Seaboard Railroad followed the Plant system and gave Tampa real rail competition. The Spanish War placed Tampa on the national map. The first World War established the shipyards. The "boom" built the modern hotels, the boulevards, and Davis Island. The second World War has given it MacDill Field and an enormously expanded shipping industry. But the town is still far from being in full stride. The measure of its future is still in incubation. The rich acres of its vast hinterland have scarcely been touched. On the far horizons slowly rise the vision of the beckoning ports of Latin America and the South Pacific.

CHAPTER 18

TAMPA WINS THE SPANISH WAR

THE Spanish War crept quietly up on Tampa.

In the early 'eighties, Don Ybor, tired of the everlasting factional differences and labor troubles that were wrecking the hand-rolled cigar industry of Key West, came to the Tampa district, looking for a new location. Don Ybor believed that if he could get his Cuban cigar workers out of the disturbing atmosphere of Key West and further away from Cuba, production would increase and his properties flourish. He proposed to bring some two thousand Cuban cigar rollers and their families along with him to a new location. Tampa had then a population of about twenty-five hundred. Bradenton, Manatee and Palmetto, clustered together on the Manatee River, looked attractive, and Don Ybor went there first, but the folks around the mouth of the Manatee would have none of the project. Angrily, Don Ybor went to Tampa, where more enterprising souls saw the point of his proposals quicker and welcomed him. Ybor City, suburb of Tampa, was born, an almost entirely Cuban

213

community, reflecting in Tampa's political and social life
every upheaval that swept Havana. Tampa grew accustomed to Cuban revolutionists; to little groups of dark-
faced, whispering men who clustered under the Spanish
balconies that overhung the business streets; to rumors
of plots and counter-plots; to gun-runing and even, time
and again, to assault and assassination. The men who
took out the *Three Brothers* and the *Dauntless,* noted
gun-runners of the early 'nineties, knew that Tampa
waterfront well, and there were many men along the
docks of the Hillsborough River who understood every
crook and cranny in the convoluted Cuban coast better
than any harbor in America except, possibly, Key West.
So the ruckus in Cuba was no great news in Tampa.

H. B. Plant had brought his Plant System railroads into
Tampa some years before and had erected the imposing
Tampa Bay Hotel, the only one in Florida that rivaled
the great hotels Flagler was building in St. Augustine.
The activities of the Plants were of infinitely greater
interest to Tampa, as 1898 rolled in, than the scurryings
of Gomez and Maceo, or the ponderous pronouncements
of the revolutionary president, Estrada y Palma. The
paving issue was in the forefront of interest. "Tampa,"
declared the "Times" editorially, "is losing $1000.00 per
day by not having her streets paved." Latin-American
trade, too, was beginning to interest Tampa shippers and
businessmen. The Plants had a line to Honduras and
another to Jamaica, and of course the *Olivette* and the

Mascotte made regular trips to Havana. When Bonacker and Bowyer, early in January, announced the building of the first important cold-storage warehouse in Tampa, to be used in developing Central-American and West-Indian trade, it began to look as if there might be something in the idea. The *Olivette* was putting on a regular excursion to Havana at about forty dollars a ticket, two and a half days' voyage, and two days in Havana, including a "cock fight in the plaza—very interesting," and sometimes a Sunday bullfight. The *Mascotte* advertised its first excursion to Puerto Cortez, Honduras, three days each way with two days in port for eighty dollars, first class. "You can certainly bring back a parrot or a monkey." Mr. and Mrs. Plant and a party of guests took advantage of the excursion and went over late in the Spring.

The *Maine* was blown up on the night of February 15th. The "Tribune" was a morning paper and caught for its regular edition the meager dispatches which first touched American soil at the little Punta Rassa cable station. The "Times," the evening paper, was tipped off, and went "extra." Neither paper had much of a wire service in those days, although both began taking a regular press service after the soldiers began to pour in.

But even then the papers were models in restraint. The "Times" gave the Maine story a one-column, three-deck head the next day in its regular edition. "Horrible Accident," said the headline. Editorially the paper urged the need for coolness and the patience to "await developments." There was no prescience in the mind of the "Times" editor that the dull rumble that doomed the *Maine* also rang the bell for a new day for Tampa.

War was not declared for almost two months after the *Maine* went down. Popular interest rose and fell with events. As late as March 30th, when the clouds of international discord were visibly daily growing blacker and the captain of the Tampa Rifles was ordering his men by advertisement to get ready with their uniforms, the arrival of the big British schooner yacht *Rhuoma* with a party of British sportsmen over for a two weeks' tarpon fishing jaunt off Passe Grille and Punta Rassa, received almost as much attention as the threats of war. But the next day the "Times" stated casually that Tampa was looming up as a possible embarkation point for the American army invading Cuba—provided that war was declared. The other possible points mentioned by the "Times" were Mobile and New Orleans. The "Times" did not refer to Jacksonville, which later on became a voluble and bitter contender for army encampments. The advantages of Tampa's location and deep harbor gave the city a great start, particularly the fact that near the harbor and railroad were large open spaces of relatively high, dry pine flats good for cantonments. Fitzhugh Lee, America's consul-general in Havana, returned home via Tampa on April 4th. The city gave him a tumultuous welcome. Two special trains with over a thousand passengers aboard, as well as a band, trundled the ten or twelve miles from Tampa to the port to welcome the doughty consul-general. One of the Maine survivors just out of a Havana hospital was pushed off his feet and under a moving train and had to be rushed into a Tampa bed. He made a quick recovery and gave away several of his uniform buttons to grateful Tampa girls.

The jostling crowd set up a tremendous roar when the stocky form of the General appeared on the pilot house deck of the *Olivette.*

"What are you yelling for?" shouted the General. "Do you want to fight?"

"Yes," roared the mob.

"That's the word I wanted to hear you say," he gustily replied. Later, talking to newspapermen, the General explained that because of his diplomatic status and the tenseness of the situation he could not talk for publication about the Cuban situation.

"But, General," persisted one reporter—for in those days reporters persisted—"do you think we can lick Spain?"

"Lick Spain?" replied the soldierly diplomat, "sure, if we go at it in the right way."

Then the General hurried away with his family and party to a private car proffered him by the Plant System. The train was a special, and quickly whirled away to Washington. Later General Fitzhugh Lee returned as commanding officer of the Seventh Corps. Congestion in Tampa was so great by then that he took the Seventh to

Jacksonville and later to Savannah, whence it embarked for the front.

Tampa's civic pulse was thumping. The War Department had agents all over the place, looking into shipping matters, sounding the harbor, checking up on local pilots, especially pilots like Captain James McKay, "who knew the Cuban coast better than he did his own bedroom." A Tampa schooner was chartered to haul two big cannons weighing fifty tons each to Key West, and when that hard job was completed the schooner took on another for the same place.

The long agonizing congressional debate was on. Despite all that Spain could do, too late for peace, the war resolution passed amid the throaty cheers of a young and naïve nation that wanted a bust and saw its chance. Mayor Gilett wired Congressman Sparkman to get busy on the encampment problem, and was advised that the congressman had seen Secretary Alger. Mayor Gilett wanted the camps located close enough to town so that the men would have easy access to the business district.

The Fifth Regiment came in early on April 18th. General Benjamin Wade and his staff followed shortly and took over command of the entire area. Two hundred and fifty acres were set aside not far from Ybor City, about a mile and a half from the center of town. Sidewalks were hurriedly built connecting the camp with the main streets. Clara Barton arrived with her Red Cross staff, en route for Key West, and waited at the Tampa Bay Hotel, which had reopened for summer business, until transportation was available. Troop trains poured in, at first one or two a day and then fifteen and thirty daily, sometimes with fifteen cars to each. Almost overnight there were twenty thousand soldiers in the Tampa district; then there were thirty thousand, then fifty thousand. Shafter arrived, then General Miles. The big lobby at the Tampa Bay exploded in a flash of golden braid, glittering sword hilts, boots bright with polish. Wide-brimmed "Stetsons" and the dark blue uniforms of the army men were the prevailing note, but here and there were monocled men in foreign uniforms, the military attachés of European nations, standing by to see what they could of the show. Also there were officers' wives and a throng of newspapermen from New York, Philadelphia, Baltimore, Washington, Detroit, Cleveland, Cincinnati and Chicago. Richard Harding Davis, Caspar Whitney, John Fox, Jr. and Frederic Remington were there—all writing their heads off.

The first and second companies of the Signal Corps departed for Sanibel Island, Key West and Tortugas, the first troops to leave Tampa, but their going made only a ripple. Volunteers were arriving from Ohio, Maryland, Michigan and New York. A detachment of colored troops under white officers was not so welcome, and there was some local trouble from Negro-baiting whites before the contingent left town for Cuba. Over in Ybor City the Cuban army was enlisting some five thousand men, most of whom were sent to join Gomez long before the American troops under Shafter got away. Captain McKay in his new ship, the *Fanita,* ran both men and guns to Gomez and in the transport *Gussie* landed a Cuban contingent and a big cargo of arms at Cardenas in one of the first battles our forces had with the Spanish army.

Early in May came the first pay-day.

"Over $175,000 was paid out yesterday," stated the "Times", "to soldiers in Tampa." The Tampa post office did the biggest money-order business in its history with the soldiers sending money back home. But all of it didn't go home.

"The storekeepers of Tampa," wrote the Washington "Post" correspondent, "are making so much money that the city banks will hardly hold it. Even a lemonade man, equipped with a bucket and two tin cups, can gross $25.00 per day."

With Shafter's arrival the brigade organization was announced. The transports began to file in. Tampa, up to now, had been a busy gulf port but never a great one. Now the long Plant System wharf was jammed with big ships, the *Gussie,* the *Berkshire,* the *Comal,* the *Allegheny* and the *Whitney.*

"Shucks," said the port captain, "this is nothing. If you'd seen the messages I saw from Sampson to Shafter last night you'd open your eyes."

In this, the last great amateur war, there was a comic fringe.

"William Astor Chanler," said the "Tribune", "has arrived with his private expedition to Cuba. Mr. Chanler is paying all of the expenses of a group of a dozen of his New York friends and if they cannot connect with the American army they will join the Cuban. It is Mr. Chanler's belief that he now has a way worked out by which he and his party can get to the front very quickly and fight the Spanish. Otherwise, he states, he will buy or charter a boat and go on and see the fun."

Two Frenchmen, Anthony Varicle and Maurice Mallet, arrived in the United States and set out for Tampa with two new type balloons which they had constructed in Paris for scouting work against the Spanish army. Shortly afterward, Epifanio Valdes, a Cuban, announced in the Tampa press his invention of a "completely new type gas airship" equipped with thirty-foot paddle wheels that would drive the seventy-foot bag two hundred miles an hour. It was equipped to alight on the water in a calm sea and make thirty miles an hour. But the conception of a directed gas bag capable of making two hundred miles an hour was far beyond the military imagination of that period, and Epifanio disappears in the clamor of immediate events. The balloon idea, however, was not entirely abandoned. In June the Signal Corps received a balloon of twenty thousand cubic feet gas capacity, and taking it to a vacant space back of the army camp, inflated it with gas from the Tampa Gas Works. The local gas, however, was too heavy and the balloon would not ascend.

"Except for that detail," observed the reporter, "the balloon test was an entire success." The balloon went on to Santiago.

Tampa had heard of the Rough Riders, and their departure from San Antonio for Tampa late in May was played up by the Tampa newspapers. Curiously enough, the actual arrival of the regiment was accepted calmly. In its modest story the "Times" mentioned neither Colonel Wood nor Lieutenant Colonel Roosevelt, and incorrectly named Major Brodie as commander. The regiment came in seven sections, with Wood in command of three and Roosevelt of four. The railroads were in such confusion that it took four days to bring the troopers into Tampa from San Antonio. Roosevelt declared he found things in a sad state.

"Everything connected with military or railroad matters was in an almost inextricable tangle," he wrote. "The railroad people unloaded us as best they could. There was no one to meet us. We had to buy the men food out of our own pockets, and seize wagons to get our spare baggage taken to the camping ground which we at last found had been allotted to us."

The cavalry outfits were generally located at Port Tampa and most of the regular United States cavalry troops were there, but Roosevelt states that when, a few days later, they received orders to embark, leaving their horses and four troops behind, they were instructed to take the train to Port Tampa at midnight. The regiment, fearful of being left behind in the confusion, reached the railroad early but could find no train. While the soldiers slept, Colonel Wood and his Lieutenant Colonel wandered about the railroad yards in search of information.

"We ran into a Brigadier General and a Major General," stated Roosevelt, "but nobody knew anything."

Then the regiment was ordered to another yard. Still no train. Finally the disgusted Rough Riders seized a passing coal train, loaded the men on, and made the port. Then came the sickening search for someone who could tell them what transport to take, where to find her, and when to line up to board her. At last Wood and Roosevelt discovered an officer who informed them they were to go on the *Yucatan*. The vessel was in midstream and Roosevelt, ascertaining that two other regiments were also assigned to the same boat, double-quicked his Rough Riders to the wharf, and, as soon as the *Yucatan* came alongside, marched his men aboard.

"The transport was overloaded, the men were packed like sardines, so at night it was only possible to walk by continually stepping over the bodies of the sleepers." The rations were bad, the "canned fresh beef was horrible stuff." There were no cooking facilities, no fresh vegetables, no ice, and the water was bad. For almost a week the *Yucatan* waited in Tampa Bay for sailing orders.

Tampa itself knew little of this. The Port was almost ten miles away. The censorship was effective if the quartermaster's department was poor, and Tampa knew only that the troops had embarked. Many believed that the fleet had already sailed.

"The government censors," related the "Tribune," "have been at work for a week attempting to create an erroneous impression as to the exact time the fleet would start. Saturday night they caused a long telegram to be sent from this place stating that the fleet had sailed last Wednesday morning and describing the departure in minute detail. Since that time telegrams have been sent from Key West stating that the fleet had arrived there."

Tampa newspapers even received dispatches from New York based on false information sent out by the censors to deceive Spanish spies, announcing that the fleet was in the Bahama channel. That was a day before the departure of the fleet from Tampa. Spies, of course, could have clustered about Tampa Bay and counted the transports on their fingers. Before the flotilla left, dispatches reached General Miles, who with his staff was at the Tampa Bay Hotel, from General Garcia near Santiago.

"Colonel Hernandez of the Cuban army," said the "Times", "arrived yesterday bringing General Miles a message from General Garcia, who commands the insur-

gent forces in the vicinity of Santiago. Garcia states he
has 9000 men well equipped. They have taken fine points
and are ready to co-operate with the U. S. Forces."

It was this message from Garcia that Shafter awaited.
With General Miles's approval, the tempo of departure
increased. The rails of the little single track railroad that
ran to the port fairly smoked from the rushing troop
trains. Thousands of soldiers stumbled over the yard
tracks and through the rank growth of jimson weed to
the dock where thirty-two transports waited.

A rumor that a Spanish gunboat had been seen off
Egmont Key startled the port for a few hours and held
up embarkation plans. Then it was discovered that the
Helena was patrolling outside the bay entrance. In a
short time two other gunboats of lighter draft came in
and took up positions off St. Petersburg. Transport after
transport swung alongside the dock and took on its contingent of shouting, cheering men. Crammed to the
bursting point, the vessels rocked in the heavy tide.
Pelicans, excited by the refuse from the overworked gal-
leys, patrolled the bay, swooping suddenly and with tremendous force to snatch floating tidbits, to the delight of
soldiers from the plains. The sun beat down, hot and
clear, the unshaded decks became frying hot. In streaks
of shade the soldiers lay in windrows, drenched with
sweat and panting like an exhausted kennel pack.

The sun, in a last arch of crimson, gold and amethyst,
was slipping toward the sharp horizon on June 13th when

the signal to depart finally came. The ships swung off two by two, led by S. S. *Miami*. The little *Hornet* acted as traffic cop and puffed busily up and down the line, getting the transports properly spaced, carrying verbal orders from flagship to captains, and generally paging the maneuver. There were thirty-six ships in all. Behind the transports came the supply craft, flanked by gunboats. With the *Miami* was the *Gussie*, an old-timer in this Cuban business, and one of the few vessels that had been under fire, and then at regular intervals came the *Comal*, the *Miller*, *Berkshire*, the *Whitney*, the *Seneca*, the *San Diego*, *City of Washington*, *Iroquois*, *Cherokee*, the *Matteawan* and many others. The busy *Olivette*, which had so frequently bustled from Port Tampa to Morro Castle and back in the piping days of peace, was a hospital ship. Off the keys awaited the *Helena*. Slowly the big vessels worked their way toward the southwest channel, the western sky turning turquoise and scarlet as the light dimmed. Behind each vessel trailed a long plume of smoke, the propellers beat steadily, a faint thrum that could be heard far inland by the citrus growers on Pinellas Point and the tomato ranchers at Terra Ceia. The farewell cheers had died; even the most ebullient trooper had ceased his raucous yells. From the flagship a stream of colored scraps spouted, the vessels slowed, swung, and then in new formation turned stiffly south toward an "unknown destination." Off to one side, skittering along, impudent and scared of official repri-

mand, were two tugs, the New York "Journal's" special
chartered boat and the New York "Sun's" *Kanapaha*. A
nation had boiled over, broken loose and was on a tear
that was to take it, like the transports, to "unknown"
destinations. The Plant executives, the boys who had
sweated and cursed over the transportation of all this
flotilla, waited at the harbor bar in the little *Mascotte*, to
give a last cheer as the fleet passed by in the darkening
twilight.

CHAPTER 19

SNAKES—SURE, SIXTY-FOOTERS

THE keys of Florida easily divide into two groups: the inner keys and outer group. Geologically their limestone formation is not different from the mainland although the Bahia Hondo group of keys, off the southeastern corner of the Florida tip of the mainland, have more of a coral base. All are overcrusted with layers of fine white sand of almost talcum white and fineness; humus; mangrove roots; sea grape; sea plume. Around Sarasota the coco palms begin to appear. Now and again in lower Sarasota Bay you will see one drooping over the waterside in the best South Sea Island manner. Around Charlotte Harbor you will find them in profusion.

Florida's history is inextricably tangled in the story of the keys. Columbus' first landfall, off San Salvador, brought the key into our American history. Ever since the keys have been the links binding our mainland to foreign shores south, southeast and southwest of us. From that day the great Gulf of Mexico-Caribbean Sea area has constantly influenced our entire national life.

Without much general recognition of the fact, this vast sweep of island-bound sea has been the American "Mare Nostrum." Our domination of it has been essential to our existence. Our naval men understood all this long before either our politicians or our economists paid any attention to it.

Along the borders of this mighty body of water our contacts with other nations press most closely. Great Britain maintains a light-buoy less than twenty flying minutes off Miami Harbor; Cuba is two flying hours away; Yucatan is slightly over three. A passenger can breakfast in Miami and eat lunch at the Strangers Club on the Cristobal-Colon waterfront.

The Navy urged the building of Fort Jefferson. The Navy recognized Key West as a vital naval center. Sloppy-minded politicians with an embryonic understanding of our entire problem of foreign relations, allowed both to sink into a shameful—almost a traitorous —desuetude. Today millions of dollars are being dumped into the limestone and coral rock of Key West in the frantic effort to make up for the years in which the naval station was allowed to disintegrate. The rehabilitation of Fort Jefferson still seems to be too great a nut for the official minds to crack. Yet Fort Jefferson is less than three hundred fifty miles from Yucatan. In terms of modern fighting planes that is about an hour's flight and less than two for a modern bomber. Yucatan, the opposing point of land thrust into the Gulf, toward Florida, has long been regarded as the ideal base for an enemy air attack upon the lower Mississippi Valley, the southeastern area, Florida and western Cuba. The great cities of Houston, New Orleans, Mobile, Pensacola, Tampa, Jacksonville and Miami, in the United States, and Havana, Cuba, all lie under the possible threat of an air attack from Yucatan. The Dry Tortugas, where the great ruin of Fort Jefferson stands, should be one of our most sensitive southwestern listening posts. In the rush of recent construction no unofficial person knows what part old Fort Jefferson is destined to play in coming events.

The Tortugas are a good two hundred miles beyond the Mangrove Coast, but the Gulf coast keys march in a long and closely integrated line. Sanibel connects with Estero and Estero is hard on the heels of Big Hickory and Little Hickory keys. The keys lie like a chain south of Naples, and studded among these innumerable keys, mangrove spits, sandbars and shallow reaches of the Ten Thousand Islands, you will find Panther, the retreat of Juan Gomez, "the last of the buccaneers," Indian, Seminole, Mormon, Pavillion, with its shining beach, Jewel, Rabbit, Porpoise, Hog, Pelican and Mosquito. From Marco south to the estuary of the Shark, the keys and keylets are beyond all number. You weave among them, in and out between rows of big mangroves often eighty feet high. Buttonwood, water oak, stunted cypress and, on the higher ground, coco and cabbage palms and a rare mahogany flourish on the larger keys. Who penetrates deeply enough into Whitefish Bay via the countless water trails will find groves of the great royal palm long ago transplanted by wind and wave from Cuba. At the Shark comes the great bend of Cape Sable, not a cape at all but almost a peninsula dotted with many capes like East Cape and Middle Cape. North of Cape Roman and Key Marco you quickly reach Sanibel, Costa, Pine and Big and Little Gasparilla, off Charlotte Harbor, and Treasure Island and Siesta Key frame the outer edge of lower Sarasota Bay, while to the north lie Longboat, Anna Maria, Egmont, Mullet, protecting lower Tampa Bay. Pass-A-Grille, Treasure and Indian beaches are on the fine keys off the St. Petersburg and Clearwater coast.

The "Cape Sable Country" is land farther from "civilization" than any other place within the continental boundaries of our country. It is the last true frontier. Leave your cruiser anchored off a key-head—slip quietly in a canoe among the hundreds of keys in the deep of the late afternoon and you are likely to flush a surprised and even indignant Cuban skipper in a small, sloop-rigged vessel, sail down, engine dead, quietly poling his way up a secret channel to some assignation. What's up —dope, Chinamen, refugees, or Bacardi? Why press the question? If you happen to know enough Spanish and must ask, put in your hail from a safe thirty yards distance. The stocky, dark-skinned fishermen will come to the stubby rail with a stock answer, "Looking for button-wood to make a little charcoal. We ran out of wood. Do you think we can get sweet water farther up?"

The Cuban would be amazed if you answered the query he fends you off with. He knows the jungles of Cape Sable keys better than any guide out of Everglades, Key West or Fort Myers. Often his shadowy sails, tinted as blue as the dusk of the late afternoon, escape as you hail, poling swiftly around the bend of the nearest key. There is always a key within twenty yards. You hear them snap on the engine and its quick bark and rumbling growl. The sloop disappears down a channel cut off by overhanging mangroves.

Smart guides do not try to follow. The Coast Guard is helpless. To know the intricate channel system of the Shark-Cape Sable country is to inherit the accumulated wisdom of the Seminoles; the lore of generations of guides. Even the best guide can easily get lost in the vast mass of keys, coon-oyster bars, clam beds and salt grass. The egrets, the pelicans, terns and gulls live in and about the keys in thousands. The little Florida deer slips among the trees on the higher land inside. Bears show themselves in the late summer and fall, and at night the harsh coughing bark of the panther and the guttural snarl of the wildcat punctuate the lonesome quacking of the waterbirds. The high thin cry of the lovely curved beak curlew is heard as flocks of them in the twilight hurry to their rookeries. In the upper reaches of the

Shark and the Harney Rivers, both of which short broad
streams act as natural drains for the Everglades, the
natives believe the web-footed panther has his lair.
Eighteen-foot gopher snakes, they say, haunt the higher
keys, driving away both the rattlesnakes and the ugly-
snouted cotton-mouth moccasin. Here, too, lives the
crocodile. It was in this general neighborhood that Buster Farrel's sixty-foot boa constrictor lurked. The story
of the great snake of the Cape Sable country is em-
bedded deep in folklore not only of the Seminoles but
also of the white settlers in that district. For years the
Cow Seminoles, who live on the Brighton reservation,
refused to venture into the Cape Sable region because
of a huge serpent which, they asserted, made that area
its habitat and chased and devoured human beings. The
Florida State Department of Agriculture, in its pamphlet
"The Seminole Indians of Florida," prepared by the Florida Writers' Project, tells the story in full and as follows:

"According to Uncle Steve Roberts of Homestead, the
serpent 'wasn't no legend but a fact. Buster Farrel, an
Indian, killed the critter in 1892,' he explained. 'Buster
was hunting when he come across a trail where the grass
was all beat down in a wide path, and thinking it was a
whopping big 'gator, he followed it. Pretty soon he
spotted the snake. It was more'n a good rifle shot from
him but he fired anyhow, and the critter went threshing
off in the grass makin' more noise than a hurricane. Buster didn't go to see whether he'd hit it or not remember-

ing the stories about the serpent swallowing Indians whole. Wasn't 'til some days later he seen a flock of buzzards flyin' around the place, and when he went down there he found the snake. The buzzards had tore and scattered the carcass so bad Buster couldn't measure it, but he swore the snake was all of 60 feet long and as big as a barrel. He cut off and kept the jaw bones, which were so big he could open them up and drop them over his body.'"

The Seminoles believed the snake lived in a lake back of Cape Sable and that this lake had an underground connection with the gulf which permitted it to make its way, in and out, between the gulf and the Everglades.

The web-footed panther may be only a legend. In the Congo country there are stories about a web-footed lion. It's a swamp-land tale. But it is easier to believe in an eighteen-foot gopher snake. The gopher is a constrictor of the black snake family, a deadly enemy of the rattler. It lives on young rats, small birds, raccoons, and rattlesnakes. I myself have seen gopher snake skins ten feet long. One topping fourteen was reported killed on Treasure Island, south of Siesta Key on Sarasota Bay, not long ago. In the steaming bog lands of the unexplored 'Glade country along the upper waters of the Shark, an eighteen-footer might very well be fact. A big gopher or black snake will clear out the rattlers half a square mile; chase away the moccasins, too, and keep all other crawling, biting vermin at a distance—all, of course, except the mosquito. The Cape Sable-Shark country breeds literally billions of mosquitoes. The 'Glades guides have to admit the mosquitoes.

"I've known men," Ed, our own guide on a recent trip, admitted, as he brought his canoe up easily to make the sharp bend about a baby key, "to all but die of suffocation from mosquitoes here in midsummer. So thick they are you don't dare breathe. They fill your nostrils and choke your nasal passages, swarm into your throat and almost kill you coughing. If you get left in this country after dark without a mosquito bar you risk your life. I know a man who was killed by mosquitoes on a mangrove key up Lossman's River just a year ago. He was literally bitten to death in a single night. He wasn't stung until he went blind, as happens in Labrador, and then starved to death. He was killed by bites in one night. He was deer hunting on the key when he lost his boat and had no way of getting off. We found him late the next afternoon. I never want to see another sight like that."

The mosquito is a short distance flyer. Except for that it would make the entire peninsula of Florida uninhabitable. Along the Mangrove Coast enlightened co-operation between the federal government and the more progressive counties is instituting mosquito control with increasingly satisfactory results. The great summer curse on all Florida within a few years will be largely eliminated. Already in some counties the mosquito pest is only a quarter of what it used to be. Cleared of the mosquito pest Florida will yet become one of the great summer resorts of the nation.

Mosquito control along the Mangrove Coast depends on drainage. All along the keys beneath and just beyond the mangrove line countless pools of water are left by the heavy rains of the late fall or early spring. The government mosquito control constructs numbers of comparatively shallow ditches that connect the beach pools with the tides. This daily flow of salt water washes away the mosquito larvae. Surface pools of rainwater are drained when possible; otherwise, especially in rural districts, oil is applied. In the cities the smaller pools, neglected cans and pans full of water, and bad backyard drainage must be watched. Florida and the whole American south are backward in mosquito control compared with Cuba, Brazil and the Canal Zone. Havana, once one of the worst of the mosquito fever-ridden ports of the world, is remarkably free of mosquitoes today. The Floridian who spends a summer vacation in Havana enjoys the cool Gulf Stream breezes sweeping through his wide open hotel windows that are entirely screenless, and goes out to the lovely summer casino or a late evening dinner on the lawn without a bite or an ankle slap to mar the entire evening. General Leonard Wood and his associates in Havana rescued Havana from the mosquito curse. No one, as yet, has done as well for any city in Florida. Public interest, however, is aroused. The possibilities of summer tourist business act as a spur. Florida may yet do for itself what other Americans were permitted to do for other people—as well as our own—in Cuba and in the great swamp area of the Panama Canal Zone.

Mosquitoes are an ancient curse. Every civilization that has grown up along the waterside has paid toll in suffering to the insects. The delta of the Nile was, and still is, one of the world's major mosquito breeding grounds. The old Egyptians, Herodotus remarks, built tall towers over the marshland. These towers were high enough to catch the off-sea evening breezes which did not touch the ground and the Egyptian marshland farmers would climb these every evening to get freedom from the pests. Egyptian fishermen wrapped themselves up in layers of fish nets. The mosquitoes could and did bite through sheets easily enough but they could not get to the flesh so well through the confusing folds of net. The early Spanish explorers along the Florida coasts suffered terribly from mosquitoes and red bugs. The chronicles of the Narváez and De Soto expeditions tell of the agonies of the Spanish soldiers, encased in coats of chain mail, plates of solid steel and leather, when the mosquitoes and red bugs managed to crawl in under steel to sting and bite to their hearts' content.

The mangrove keys in the Shark River country are often so close together that the narrow channels seem more like creeks than parts of a tidal estuary. Only the rush of the tide as it laps and curls off the sides of your boat makes it plain that you are not in some sluggish southern creek. The big mangroves with twenty-four-inch trunks stretch nearly across the passageways and in the splotched sunlight you can see how the tangled mass of mangrove, cypress and buttonwood roots make a floor over which a wildcat can easily creep or a bear or raccoon run. Impassable treacherous country for even the most cat-footed " 'Glades Cracker."

The twisting roots of the mangrove are like snakes in the half light.

"Still not so many here as you might think," says Ed as he swings the cruiser sharply over an oyster shell bank and points it down a narrow lane of overhanging boughs. "I haven't smelt a cottonmouth or a rattler all day."

"Can you smell a snake?" I asked. Snake smelling is an old story all over Florida but is still not credible to an office-bound northerner.

"Sure I can smell 'em," says Ed. "A rattler smells like an old sweaty shirt. A cottonmouth smells the same only stronger. It's a mean stink and if the snakes are aroused and mad, it gets thicker and meaner.

"It's the black snakes that keep off the rattlers," says Ed. "In the 'Glades I'd rather have a good bull black snake around me than a hound dog. Hound dogs just seem to attract rattlers. I think that rattlers hate dogs. A hunter can go plowing through a palmetto bunch and unless he steps on a rattler, it will pretty surely slide

off to one side and get away. Rattlers don't go round
looking for people to bite. If you step on a rattler he'll
coil and strike but not otherwise unless he's scared, or in
the spring when he's shedding and nervous and doesn't
see too well. But rattlers will lay for the dogs and strike
at them when they are in the air jumping through the
scrub. If a dog is bitten in the legs and you have serum
with you they get mighty sick but they can be saved.
I've carried a setter across my shoulders for six or eight
miles many a time to get him back to a vet. I've lost a
lot of dogs too. We lose a dozen dogs a year back of Fort
Myers in the bird season because of the reptiles. That's
why we like black snakes."

The sun was slipping swiftly away in heaped up amethyst and purple clouds, a huge ball of Chinese lacquer
red on the edge of the gulf. The water turned to a deep
olive green. Ahead, bobbing in the water, were a herd of
manatee, their sleek, round brown heads glistening for
an instant in the sun's last rays. A tarpon, an honest-to-
goodness big one, suddenly rose from the water close to
one side, looked at us with stony impassivity out of his
great staring eye, and curved back into the water again
with but hardly a ripple to mark the spot. The curlews,
their white backs shining in the sun's rays, were coming in,
and high above them, their wings thrumming like propeller strokes, flew a formation of black mallards.

We were deep into Whitefish Bay behind Cape Sable

and south of the Shark. In the galley the cook was working the Flit gun before dropping a can of soup into the
hot water.

Ed's mind was still on snakes.

"I saw a black snake fight a rattler once," he said. "It
was back of the Miakka River in lower Sarasota
County. I was riding the line for a big cow outfit.
Another fellow was with me. Meanest fight I ever saw,"
he continued. "We were up alongside a gully looking for
a bunch of calves and I stopped to roll a cigarette. I heard
a sort of a swishing, down in the bottom ten feet below
me, and I looked down. Then I signaled my friend to
lean over and look too.

"There was a black snake around five feet long but not
very thick. He had two wraps around the neck of a rattler. The rattler wasn't as big, maybe a foot less in size,
but he was fighting hard. Both were about ten inches up
in the air swinging back and forth. The rattler had only
three inches of free way for his head and he was waving
around trying to get a fang into the black snake's back.
Every little while the black snake would stiffen and then
plunge the rattler's head into a little slimy mud hole
round which they were fighting. The black snake was
trying to hold the rattler's head in under the muck—
trying to smother him probably. The rattler whipped
about desperately to get loose and would finally break
through enough to get his head up again. Then the performance would be repeated. Pretty soon we noticed a

second snake lying stretched out on a warm flat stone about ten feet away watching the battle with complete absorption. It was probably a female. None of the snakes paid the slightest attention to us. The terrific wrestling match continued for another ten minutes. The rattler's efforts grew weaker. It was plain to be seen that the rattler couldn't last much longer. The black snake jammed the rattler's head in the mud and it didn't even try to come up. Its body slackened off and got pretty limp but the black snake held on for at least another five minutes. Then it let loose and the rattler lay motionless on the sand and mud. The black snake shook itself, coiled and struck at the rattler's back, pulling its head out of the mud. And then, by Jing, that darned black snake swung around to the rattler's head, opened its mouth and started to swallow that rattler whole. A full six inches was gone as we had to pull out. The other snake just lay there and watched. Never moved."

Down in the galley the cook was still fussing with his pans. Twilight is a matter of a few very brief minutes in the Shark River country in March, and Ed was pushing the cruiser into the stream intending to spend the night offshore.

"Blows the 'skeeters' and gnats away," he said. "Anyhow we want to get an early start for Harney Creek and Lossman's River and if we are out in the gulf we can get away on the fly with the first break of dawn."

Snake talk, however, still continued. The guides

grouped round the stern were muttering among themselves while Ed outlined the next day's program.

"I feel as you do, Ed, about black snakes," said one, "but I don't go along on gopher snakes. I kill gophers every time I see 'em and I've seen a plenty. I favored gophers along with black and king snakes until I saw one killed and opened up once. It was back of Fort Myers and it must have been over twelve feet long. It had ten baby quail in its stomach and that settled it for me. Black snakes chase rats and other varmints and while I've seen a king in a blackbird nest once in a while, going after the eggs, yet kings are such terrible poison on diamond backs and cottonmouths, I wouldn't hurt a king if I could help it, but I'm off gophers."

George, down in the galley, despite the music of his pots and pans had been following the conversation. He broke in suddenly.

"I saw a gopher swallow a puppy once," he said.

"I was doing a bit of farm work on the upper Miakka River. We was just finishing up milking when we heard the damnedest squalling and squawking you ever heard back of the corn crib. We hustled back and found a big gopher with a three-months-old hound pup in its jaws doing his best to gulp him down. One of the boys grabbed a heavy field hoe and hit the gopher about a foot back of his neck and cut him in two. A minute later the puppy got loose but he was a terrible scared pup. Yes sir, I think gophers is almost as bad as 'gators around game and stock."

It might be inserted here that "Texas Jim" Mitchell who has hunted and sacked literally thousands for zoo and laboratory purposes—Jim being one of the big producers of venom for rheumatism—thinks rather highly of the rattler.

The rattler gives a warning and rattles, Jim points out, and the Florida rattler behaves himself—outside of dogs —and is slow to strike.

"The rattler is no nervous reptile. Step on him, and unless he's already irritated by something else, the chances are twenty to one he won't strike. He'll coil. His neck and head will be twisted in that deadly 'S' formation that precedes a strike. But he'll hold his head back and mouth closed. Out will flash the rather thick, black, split tongue, the antenna by which the snake hears, his head will sway slightly and the frenetic whine of the thrumming rattles will take on a shriller note but that is all. Touch him a second time and he still will not strike. The head will sway; the tongue will flash in and out, out and in. The whole diamond-marked brown and dun orange mass will slowly revolve, coming around with the deadly deliberation of a great three-rifled turret on a modern battleship. The snake's nose, the flashing antenna, have done their work well. The snake knows where the enemy lies. Its head is aimed directly at it.

Touch it again. There is a blur; a split second's view of the open jaws and the head is back again; swaying like that of a boxer, the muscles of the neck and the body as rigid as coiled steel; the body cocked in the 'S' position seeking, searching for the point of attack. The rattles are keening, the air is full of the telltale musky odor of old clothes or cucumbers. The squat pointed head with the bulging pouches over the jaws moves in an almost invisible beat to some rhythm that only Master Rattler can hear. With no further disturbance the head will slowly drop down to the first fold, the body relaxes, the under coils flatten out into a deep triangular shape, the tenseness departs and the reptile will soon go to sleep."

It is pretty nearly impossible for a rattler to strike above the eighteen-inch line. Most strikes land between eight and ten inches from the ground. Good, strong heavy hunting boots suffice therefore on excursions. Bad strikes above the boot top may come when the hunter is stooping over to pick up a bird or crouches to hide from approaching game.

A Florida hunter may go through an entire season without seeing a rattler, copperhead or moccasin. The moccasins are more numerous than the others but are a slow and sluggish snake. Frequenters of marshy ground, they are held in less respect than the rattler by the "Crackers" who know most about them. I have talked to men who have hunted the Florida jungles year after

the bigness of a great spaniell, which for want of a har-
quebuz he durst not attempt to slay."

The rattlesnake, Mr. End says, is one of the cleanest
animals in the world. Its poison glands are entirely separated from the rest of its body and once the head is removed the body is as innocent of poison as "the body of
a lamb." The rattlesnake is a discriminating eater. It
will consume only live animals—cottontail rabbits being
its favorite food—and only eats four or five of them a
year. So positive is its dislike of anything dead that a
rattlesnake will not even crawl over the body of a dead
animal.

"We use about a thousand a year," says Mr. End.
"We could use two thousand. They weigh between six
and ten pounds each on the average. Ten pounds is very
good." They come to the factory alive in sacks.

Rattlesnake meat, Mr. End went on, is generally pink
in color, has no fat and tastes a good deal like the breast
of quail. It is, he asserts, crammed full of all the vitamins.

"And why not? The snakes live on the best of food
and spend all day lying out in the warm Florida sun
doing nothing but absorbing vitamins."

Some people like their rattlesnake straight, just boiled
and canned; others like it smoked.

"But how do they eat it?" I asked.

"Oh," says Mr. End, "some use it in salad and others
as a spread. It's nice as a spread."

"Is it?" I said. "Who eats most of it?"

"I don't know," says Mr. End. "Clubmen and swells."

Perhaps the eighteen-foot black snakes aren't quite eighteen feet. Perhaps the web-footed black panther is more story than fact. There are plenty of things about the Everglades that every hunter and trapper from the little settlements deep inside know about, and cannot explain.

Ghost fires for instance. The most talkative of the "Crackers" admit you do not see them often. Few people not of the Everglade folk have ever seen them at all. A few of the "sports" and "outsiders" have, though. The "Crackers" and "outsiders" alike tell the same story.

Always it is on a dark night that the fires occur. They are always on the horizon; sometimes they appear in great belching waves, scarlet to yellow, heaving and tossing, or again, the fires appear like a single, straight solid column reaching from the tops of the palms straight into the skies. No noise. No crackling. No smell of smoke. Just a bright, unearthly radiance and a vast stillness. Then they fade out as if a giant hand were slowly dimming down the wick. Tremendous outbursts of marsh gases have been advanced in explanation. Some electrical disturbance, say others. About the crocodiles there is no dispute. That there were colonies of this most ruthless and savage type of saurian in the Florida marshes was scientifically established sixty years ago, but because of their rarity compared with the infinitely more numerous " 'gator" the fact that crocodiles live in the United States is scarcely realized.

The alligator is at best an unpleasant creature. Its habits and its appetites are, to be conservative, repulsive. Out in the swamps or along the edge of the woods, in the early evening, its hoarse, muffled bellow chills the skin of any but the hardened Cracker. The alligator kills and eats a great many fish for some reason; mostly gar-fish and other piscatorial debris. He takes an occasional turtle, shell and all, and there is no question but that he loves young duck, all sorts of water birds, any animal almost that he can easily and safely seize, haul under water, drown. He allows his prey a few days to soften up and decay, then he swallows it. The stories about 'gators taking young pigs and lambs, even calves which wandered too far into the jungle country and got too close to the water, are many. And out of the welter of stories of 'gators attacking men and women—and children—possibly some are true. But attacks upon human life by alligators in the swamp country back of the Mangrove Coast are certainly rare. In every community there are plenty of men who think nothing of diving into a pool where alligators lurk, to grapple, throw them about and capture them. Keep clear of the terrific smash of their wonderful tails and you are fairly safe.

On the other hand, the crocodile is a bad and dangerous egg from every angle. In appearance the crocodile and the alligator are generally similar. Their habits and feeding grounds are the same. They are often together in the same holes in the streams or in the quieter ponds or wallowing pools in the cypress bays in the swamps.

The crocodile can and does very effectively swing open both jaws, while the lower jaw of the alligator is fixed and rigid. The crocodile is of a lighter green color, almost olive green at times. The outstanding difference between the alligator and the crocodile is the nose, that of the crocodile markedly the more pointed.

The alligator is more or less a timid, retiring soul, asking for little beyond its daily menu of fish. The crocodile is a ruthless and savage go-getter.

The crocodile will attack anything that it can hope to set its vicious rows of teeth into or smash with its fiercely swinging tail. It will lunge at a man, track a child along a swamp path and even lie in wait for its return. The crocodile will instantly attack a man precipitated into water by the overturn of a canoe. Many have been known to follow men upon islands and bars and rush at them in fierce and burning ardor to sink their jaws into their flesh.

Fortunately few of them are left in Florida. One was shot lunging across a narrow pond to get at a child playing along the banks a few years ago, down on the southern keys. It was unusually large, nearly a fourteen-footer, and it took two bullets from a .30-.30 rifle, under the forward left leg, to bring it down in the shallow of the pond. There used to be a great many more of both crocodiles and 'gators and, because they were so often confused and all called alligators, it may be that many bloody deeds charged against the 'gator were really sins of the crocodile.

The range of the crocodile was always less extensive than the alligator's in Florida. Some experts think the crocodile was never more than a visitor among the swamps and streams behind the Mangrove Coast.

CHAPTER 20

CORN IS THEIR TIPPLE

RANDY was boss of a prosperous cafe but he was not at all happy. Leaning over the long beautifully polished rosewood bar he studied the communication from his liquor wholesalers in Tampa; an enclosure from the Treasury agents of Uncle Sam and an opinion, brief and to the point, from his attorney. Another liquor tax was on. His but to pay it. The tax went on at midnight. The mark-up in the prices would have to begin at once. The bottle customers would get the bad news the next morning. How the bar consumers would growl at the increase in the cost of their drinks Randy hated to consider. War was hell in the liquor business.

He walked over to the tall shelves where the bottles rested like books in some old-fashioned library. Slowly scratching his chin he took down the old price labels and wrote in the new ones.

"Four-fifty," he said, "five-fifty to six-fifty. Getting awful high. The Revenue boys had better look out. There's going to be a lot of blue smoke over the hammocks."

But Randy was wrong about blue smoke. Blue smoke is old stuff and the boys who run the stills in the hammocks along the Mangrove Coast tolerate no blue smoke nor any other kind in their operations today.

"Nix on the smoke," said the Boy Moonshiner. The Boy Moonshiner looked like a well-put-together junior at Gainesville; his clothes were distinctly campus cut, but his only laboratory had been the big black stewing pots and the slender coiled copper worm of the "still" back in the hammocks. Now, he told me, he was "through with running the juice."

"I've got a business," he said briefly. "And besides that," he continued, "in the sixteen years that I've been in and out of the stills I've seen a lot of money made but I never saw a single moonshiner keep a worthwhile wad. Over half of the boys I knew who were big shots in running liquor along the gulf coast during prohibition are on relief right this minute. A few of them are still at it, hustling 'smoke' in the Negro sections at a dollar-fifty a gallon and just getting by. Some of the boys who ran the boats in from Bimini are still fooling around bringing in Chinamen and a load of heroin now and again, but that's terribly dangerous, and in the end, the money isn't big enough. Some went back to farming. They figure their AAA checks will give 'em a big enough cash crop to buy store stuff—that with a month or two of work on the WPA. But with red whisky going to over two dollars a 'fifth,' things may pick up. The boys

off the back lands want their whisky and they can't pay
two to four dollars a bottle on a thirty-dollar a month pay
check—not and keep their folks together."

The Boy Moonshiner went on. "Smoke," he said, "is
obsolete. The old Cracker that taught me how to make
my first run told me that they burned corncobs up in
north Georgia, but down here on the coast we use gasoline burners. No smoke at all to bring the wrong people
round; easy to operate and much hotter and faster than
even fat pine."

On the gulf coast, says the Boy Moonshiner, the matter of the location of a still was never difficult. The great
outer fringe of swamp land encircling the 'Glades was
too close; the vast stretches of prairie land, studded with
"bay heads" bristling with dense cypress and palm
growth, were easy of access.

"It's best never to be over five or six miles from town,"
he said.

"There is only one really dangerous time in handling
a load of liquor and that's when you take it to town. The
shorter the haul, the better. On the road people see you.
If they note that you come along every few days with a
load behind you, they begin to talk. Or you have an
accident and spill a lot of whisky on the pavement.
A hundred things can happen to you bringing it in. So I
always kept my still close in.

"It's almost impossible to keep a still in safe operation

in a town," he went on. "It's the smell of the mash. It seems that you can do nothing about it. You can pretend you are making up a hog feed or something for the chickens, and that may stifle neighborhood gossip for a week or two, but it always gives you away in the end. Someone is bound to recognize the acrid yet musty alcoholic odor of the discarded mash, and talk—perhaps to the sheriff, perhaps simply at the corner store. But sooner or later a deputy gets wind of it and drops round. And then, even if no arrest takes place, the velvet is out of the game. Paying off sheriffs or policemen or special prohibition people is almost as bad as paying a tax," he said. "Overloads the business and keeps you on the jump all the time," was how he put it.

"I never paid the federal prohibition men a penny," he said. "The federals never caught up with me because I operated small stills and they were looking for the big men. All I ever had to fork over was five dollars or ten dollars a delivery in one or two counties. Once in a while I gave a cop a ten-dollar bill or maybe a gallon of extra good stuff. When you work it on that basis you are safe enough."

The situation is tougher now, according to the Boy Moonshiner. It's sugar trouble. Sugar is the base in making " 'shine." It's the essential ingredient. The federal government lately makes a sharp check on all sugar purchasers. All wholesalers and dealers in sugar are expected to keep watch. Any unusually large purchases by strange customers, or any too-regular purchases made by people whose need of sugar is not obvious, are supposed to be reported to the officials. Of course the war time sugar restrictions have about doubled this trouble.

"Lots of people don't know how the government keeps tabs now," he said, "but it's a fact, and it makes the work of maintaining your runs regularly, which is very important, a lot more difficult than it was a few years ago. The men who operate the big five-hundred and thousand-gallon stills are specially hit., They need lots of sugar and sometimes they can't keep it coming in quantities big enough to insure steady production. Hauling in too much sugar sets the revenue men looking around, and that leads to raids. I know one big thousand-gallon still up back of Tampa that was picked up because of its sugar trail."

The Boy Moonshiner thought maybe he could beat the sugar situation himself though. He had contacts. Some small fruit and tomato canners, friends of his, would always let him have a few hundred-pound sacks. There was no close check at all on the canners. Also he knew a sugar leak in Miami. He had heard too of a retired rum runner operating a schooner between Cuba and a point south of Fort Myers, and bringing in sugar, sans quota, sans duty.

"That fellow takes his schooner over to a spot west of Havana, not so far from one of the centrals. He gets his raw sugar from a friend, who sacks it for him and

delivers to the boat. He can carry a good jag of it and
at the price he buys it in Cuba he can make a pretty
profit. No one ever bothers him. Anyhow most of his run
is at night. He takes care of a couple of fellows who
have big stills back of Miami. One other man is on the
boat with him and I'll bet he's clearing better than
seventy-five hundred dollars a year. It's one of the neat-
est things on the coast, but of course, it's only good if
you have the connections fixed at both ends. It's not a
wide open market like whisky was while the country
was dry.

"One of the nicest things in the world to operate is a
fifty-gallon still." There was a warm reminiscent glow
in the boy's brown eyes as he spoke. He seemed to be
seeing the cluster of big smoke-blacked pots among the
palms on the high-up hammock; the standing boiler of
the cooker with its peaked top and the copper tubing
leading from it to the elevated stand where the water
barrel stood. The fine coiled length of copper tubing in
which the hot alcoholic vapor was reduced to liquid
again, and the trickle of colorless liquid into the waiting
can, was pleasant to think about. If you are careful and
clean and have any of the instincts of a good house-
keeper, he went on, you can make a nice run off a fifty-
gallon still—easily five gallons of good 'shine per run.
Commercially, you needed to work on a rougher basis.
You would have to make at least ten or twelve runs a
week to make it worth while, but the Boy Moonshiner

was smiling over the joy of pure amateur effort—no illegal distribution, just production of fine 'shine for oneself.

"Just yourself," he said, "and once in a while for a few of your friends. It wouldn't be hard and I guess it isn't illegal if you do it that way. And there isn't any whisky like good corn-meal 'shine if it's cooked right and you give it time to age.

" 'Shine," he said, "is not much good if it's less than six months old; and it should be kept in a good charred oak barrel. Not every barrel, even if it is charred, is good to age 'shine in," he said. "But a man who knows his way about barrels can pick the good ones. If the 'shine is soundly sloshed about every few days, something mighty appetizing in the way of whisky will appear at the end of six months. Not enough of the real six-month stuff gets on the market." The talk about ten-year-old 'shine was tall moonshine, he added. Though he once had had, he said, a gallon of 'shine that was honest to God, twenty years old. It came to him as an inheritance from an uncle in North Carolina.

"I sipped from it for a year," he said. His eyes glistened. "It ran over your tongue like sugar water. It seemed to almost evaporate before it hit your gullet. But pretty soon you felt it warm in your stomach. I suppose that was the finest 'shine in the world. My own 'shine was good but I never drank it. When you still it for distribution you should never drink."

However, said the Boy Moonshiner, returning to his original theme, if you made it just for yourself, three or four runs a year, never touching a run until it was at least a year old, there certainly could be no valid objection to a man's drinking his own stuff. The development of a still in every kitchen would be an excellent thing, he said, for the national morale. Everybody would get better liquor, it would be healthier and safer, and people would drink at home and enjoy it more.

"Why," he said, "it would be just like eating a cake at home. Mother's cakes were always better'n those you bought at a bakery. It would be the same in 'shine. That would be the trouble though. So many people would go to cooking their own 'shine and drinking in their own kitchens that the government couldn't stand it. The government would lose so much money in taxes. Probably millions. You can't keep on spending money like they are doing now without you get lots of jack off the taxes. And that means whisky."

"It's always been whisky that carried the government," propounded the Boy Moonshiner. "Not so long ago whisky was about all that carried it. Whisky paid for the army and the navy and all the congressmen and the senators, but they have outspent whisky lately. So you see the government couldn't stand for a lot of people having their own private stills. We all have got to do our drinking in bars to keep up the government nowadays."

He had more to say about how the Florida gulf coast country was never especially noted for its 'shine. After sixteen years of active operation, he concluded that Florida moonshine, when properly stilled and aged, was as fine as any made in the country. The Florida product was well up to any produced in the stills of the Carolinas, or down Sandy Creek Valley in Kentucky, or in the mountains of east Tennessee.

"That stuff they boil out over around Memphis," he observed, "was and is the worst in the world. That's the poison they sell down that Beale street, which sets off the colored folks in big razor rows. They still good 'shine in east Tennessee but not much gets over to the Mississippi river.

"The old fellow who taught me how to put it up told me that the best 'shine cooker there ever was lived in western South Carolina. He made whisky over there for a long time and had a select trade—only judges, lawyers and barbers. He sold his customers direct. He never sold anything that was less'n four years old. But one night he and his brother got into a fight and a guy was killed. He had to beat it out to northern Wyoming and live in a cave in the hills and make 'shine for the cowboys. No one ever bothered him out there. He wrote my old boss and told him it was a nice place but that the cowboys wanted a handful of dry peaches put into every barrel. That colored it up and they liked the taste that way, but the old man said he didn't think it improved it any. Out in Wyoming four dollars a gallon was the price. During the boom down here," the Boy said, "I have sold two-day-old 'shine in two-gallon jugs at eighteen dollars per jug but that was out of line and didn't last long. In the 'dry' time you could get four to six dollars a gallon and sometimes a little more if you had a good product and knew your people. With the bigger stills the cost per gallon is quite low and the big distilleries must get the cost way down—maybe fifty cents a gallon. Of course I'm not including their bottles or advertising or aging overhead. That's just my estimate, but I know I could produce it for a dollar even if I aged it six months. In fact, 'shine sells around three dollars a gallon now although the stuff they sell in the jungles is priced as low as a dollar-twenty-five to two dollars. The hot spots will retail that poison at ten cents a shot and three shots will send you out foaming.

"If you have a nice private line of customers and can afford to let your 'shine mature for a year you can count on a steady trade at four dollars a gallon, but a line like that takes years to build up. And of course, there is always a risk."

On the Florida gulf coast, the Boy Moonshiner thought there was probably two hundred thousand gallons of moonshine produced each year. The whole state, he believed, produced over a million. The federal government was increasingly active, which cut the production. With the price of "fancy" whisky rising (and any whisky produced by a legal distillery and sold in a labeled bottle was "fancy"), he thought production would go up sharply. "It will," he said, "if they can fix it to get the sugar."

Taxes, he repeated, largely made the whisky market. Aging was the big problem. There was no real substitute for time, although putting the new stuff into charred barrels and giving it a long ride over a rough road in a truck was considered a helpful substitute. However, that was often dangerous, he pointed out. Some of the boys strained theirs through a couple of pieces of carpet, and held that that aged it overnight. One man he knew used to strain it through several lengths of yarn, letting it drip from one skein to another. Good material made good 'shine. For a fifty-gallon still, you needed thirty pounds of the best crushed corn meal, and with this at least fifty pounds of sugar. You had to be sure you had the best of soft water.

On the gulf coast the water problem is a bad one because so often our water has sulphur in it or a trace of salt. Good 'shine must be made out of good water. As a rule you can get good water twenty to thirty feet. But if you are located too close to the gulf you are always likely to get a taint of sulphur or salt. Put your meal into your cooking pot along with the sugar, stir it up and then cover it with water. It will start fermentation soon. If you are in a hurry heat your water and fermentation will start a lot earlier. Let it bubble for at least six days; then skim off the foam and draw off the liquid. Leave the mash there. The second and third run off the mash produces a better whisky than the first run but for every run you've got to add another fifty pounds of sugar. That's why sugar is so important. Pour the liquid into the boiler and keep the fire slow. Use a gasoline burner for this fire, is the boy's recipe, although lots of cooks say a charcoal fire is better. The fire must be kept fairly low. The stuff shouldn't boil up for at least an hour and a half. The steam will go through the coil and cool back into liquid. The run should be about a gallon every twenty minutes. Rye runs about the same except that rye ferments a great deal more actively. Down on the coast corn is standard, although the boys always made a few rye runs to take care of the odd customers. Some of them were very odd, he said.

"Outside of the litter of folks that crowd into Palm Beach in the Winter, no one ever heard of Scotch until prohibition, and it never was very popular along the Florida gulf coast. Of course, the northern tourists brought a demand for it and the boys operating between here and Bimini and Havana brought it in. I got hold of a consignment of Scotch mash once and put it through, but did not do so well with it. It had a kick; it had alcohol and it certainly wasn't corn but we couldn't sell it for Scotch. It's my guess that our water wasn't just right for it or perhaps my timing wasn't so good. One of the boys tried to make a run with apricots once, but it was terrible. Another tried plums and blew up his still. Anyhow corn is our natural. After all, it's America's greatest contribution to the business of drinking—and that's one of the great businesses of the world. The gulf-coaster wants 'corn'—not Bourbon, not rye, not Scotch, just good 'corn.' When he is in his party clothes he will fool around and pretend he is crazy after cocktails but take the northerner away and you couldn't sell a cocktail a day in most of the bars down here. Corn is his tipple—corn with just a trace of the original kernel; the very sniff of it brings up the memory of the old barnyard, the cows and the chickens; corn that's pale yellow and slides down your throat like hot butter, that's their native drink down here and it's one to be proud of.

"I don't suppose I'll ever run another still," said the Boy Moonshiner. "That is, not commercially. My mother doesn't like it and there's no glamour and excitement in the business any more. It's just a crooked business now —like selling policy tickets. But I've still got the hankering to make a run on my own some time, just for myself, and make the finest batch of 'shine that was ever made. I'd get me the best corn meal, the sweetest sugar and the softest spring water. I'd get it tested and all of that. Make the finest mash and let it ferment until the foam is stiff and high and the liquid almost hops out of the pot. I'd give it a full three runs and try to squeeze out about twenty gallons. Then I'd hunt up just the right barrel, one that's been charred at least a year but never used. I'd put my 'shine away in the haymow and keep it there for the next ten years—but hell, how do I know where I'll be in the next ten years?"

CHAPTER 21

THIS HOLLOW SPHERE

DR. CYRUS R. TEED was a skeptic.

Born in 1839 on a farm at a place where the road widened out, Teedville, New York (later Trout Creek), he took to the medical profession as soon as a country school education would let him, studied with an uncle, and began practice in Utica. The Civil War closed down upon him as upon thousands of others. He served as a surgeon in the Union armies and then returned to private practice.

Home from the batter and crash of war his own natural-born doubting instincts boiled and bubbled. Dr. Teed wanted to know. He wanted to find the answers for himself—answers that would satisfy.

Now, the Bible, for one thing. In the 1870's the Bible was a very definite and personal thing in the lives of many Americans. It was an intimate part of family life. Resting on the parlor center table it was a visible and physical reminder of the power of the Almighty and his direct interest in the affairs of every member of the family.

Teed began to doubt. He engaged in lengthy research, going deep into authorities which, dusty and dull as they may seem to us now, were primed with controversy as old as history. His search was for the Truth. Probing into the lore of the theologians, the Churchmen and the Schoolmen, he ran up against a problem of science—the Copernican System.

Wasn't it all based on guesswork, after all? he reasoned as he struggled with the problems that tumbled about him as he bored into the strong walls of the old Pole's philosophy.

Did Copernicus really prove anything? Was his hypothesis really subject to any greater degree of proof than those of a dozen other "scientists"?

Wasn't it simply that Copernicus had secured the doctor's nod at a time when politically, ecclesiastically, and economically it was a sound thing to give the weight of "authority" to the old Pole? Or wasn't it?

Teed worked hard on that one.

Struggling down the Copernican trail, Dr. Teed was bitten with another idea.

"All life develops from cellular forms or conditions," he said. "Nature is uniform, life in the aggregate must conform to the same general laws. The Universe must conform."

The Universe, thought the Doctor. The Universe; then the Earth. And then Dr. Teed made a discovery that to him—and to a goodly number of others—was conclusive. He became convinced by the chain of his own reasoning that the earth was a hollow globe—that the inhabitants of the earth did not live on the outside of the globe, held tidy and tight by the law of gravitation, but on the inside. He declared the earth to be a hollow globe of twenty-five thousand miles circumference, with the sun, the moon, and all the stars contained inside.

In 1896, near Naples, Florida, a geodetic expedition, organized and equipped by Dr. Teed, manned by disciples of the Doctor, took the apparatus required for his experiment. On the flat sands of the gulf beach, they conducted the experiments and proved the case—to their satisfaction.

The curvature of the earth, declared the Doctor, was up, not down.

But this simplification was only made later. During the years following the Doctor's discovery of "cellular cosmogony," and while he was still formulating the principle in his mind, he drifted into mental healing. He became a leader in the organization of mental healers. He opened offices; lectured throughout the country, established a magazine. And as he worked upon the theories of cellular cosmogony, and edited his magazine, Dr. Teed also took a look at the economic system. The competitive system, he asserted, was an outgrowth of paganism, a "form of economic cannibalism." He foresaw world-wide revolution as a consequence. Human relations, he declared, must go back to the primitive base of the early Christian church where all goods were held in common. This belief in the need of a social system based upon collective ownership led to the organization of the Koreshan Unity, a group which was to work out these principles in daily life. The Unity was first located at College Place, Chicago, then it moved into the suburbs. But society in the up and competing Middle West was not friendly.

1893 was World's Fair year in Chicago. Many men from far places visited the city. Among them was a real-estate dealer from Fort Myers. He met Dr. Teed and described the Charlotte Harbor area so convincingly that Dr. Teed made the trip to the rail-head at Punta Gorda and took a sloop to Fort Myers. After an extensive investigation he accepted the proposal of a resident who agreed to deed a large tract near the gulf and drained by a stream, if he would establish a colony on the land. The first group of colonists, twenty-four of them, arrived in February, 1894, and began the heart-breaking labors inevitable to pioneers in virgin land. The grubbing of the palmettoes, clearing the underbrush and trees, fighting off the hordes of mosquitoes, midges, red bugs, sand flies and fleas, again and again almost broke down the little company's morale, but Teed's leadership was still vital, his vision kept them going. A log house was finally erected, the fleas were routed, kitchens were built, and life began to come up to the dream. In December, 1896, Dr. Teed's geodetic expedition arrived. The time had come to put the Theory to test.

Upwards of a dozen men were in the party. The noon high sun beat down on the glittering sand shore. The surface of the gulf, level and undisturbed as a mirror, lay blue and green. To one side were piles of curious looking objects of wood. They looked like sections of a light fence. On closer examination they seemed to be double T-squares. They composed Dr. Teed's rectilineator. With them he expected to prove that the earth's surface was not convex and constantly falling away from any given point but, on the contrary, concave and rising upwards. The Doctor had reasoned it all out during the dark nights of the winter of 1869 and 1870, a quarter of a century before.

For some weeks previous to the beginning of the geodetic operations two fifteen-foot two-by-six-inch perpendicular stakes had been set out upon the beach. They marked the points along the line of the Koreshan community's first survey to determine to their satisfaction the true contour and ratio of curvature of the earth's surface. From the fixed stake on the approach to the Naples dock the stakes marked the direction of the meridian line. Standing in a long line were lesser stakes that indicated shorter intervals of space. A survey had been made along the coast with the usual surveyors' instruments, and the line had been measured along which the rectilineator was to be moved section by section, in precise adjustments, for four and a half miles down the coast.

As the air line was to be straight and the shore line was irregular, excavations were necessary, and all obstructions were cleared away.

"The leveling of the first section was the point for the exercise and application of the greatest skill and accuracy," states the Koreshan booklet "The Cellular Cosmogony," which reports the test in detail. "The first section must be accurately leveled. For this purpose we obtained the finest and most sensitive spirit levels obtainable. In connection with this we had our twelve-foot mercurial geodetic level, invented specially for this survey. Being twelve feet in length it was susceptible of being used with great accuracy and precision. Applied to the first section the spirit and the mercurial levels agreed."

At 8:50 in the morning of March 18th, 1897, the leveling was concluded and pronounced perfect by the staff working on the problem. From then on the line was projected on the basis of the principles upon which the test was based.

Carefully and patiently for eight weeks the staff worked along the line south of the Naples dock, checking and cross-checking—careful, tedious and trying work.

At the end the staff believed that they had proved their case. The curvature of the earth's surface, they declared, was *up* not down. "Cellular Cosmogony" will give you all the mathematical details of the measurements, much too intricate for this slight review. But to the members of the Koreshan colony the test rendered their position impregnable.

"The Universe," the Koreshan Unity believe, "is an egg or shell, obtaining as a structure perpetually recreative and existent."

Within this shell there are "three distinct domains of stars and three distinct atmospheres." The stars, they say, are not worlds "but focal points of substance or centers of combustion." They do not believe the planets are inhabited.

Other experiments were tried in time. None so completely convinced Dr. Teed and his adherents as the four-mile survey.

Satisfied himself, Dr. Teed made no passionate effort to enforce his theory upon the world. The Koreshan community accepted it. The world could take its own time discovering the truth. The community meanwhile slowly grew; its saw-mill prospered and the earlier log houses gave way to well-built tropical houses.

Dealing like communists among themselves the Koreshanians dealt on a competitive basis with the outside world. They sold their lumber and fine nursery stock from their extensive gardens, vegetables, berries and truck. The community was in no sense isolated. Its members took a keen interest in local affairs, and now and then injected themselves into county politics, and the solid vote of the Unity voters became a political weapon of real force. To protect their interests they established "The American Eagle," a weekly newspaper. Its editor today, A. H. Andrews, a pioneer in the colony, is recognized as one of the ablest editorial writers in Florida weekly journalism.

In December, 1908, at the age of sixty-nine, Dr. Teed died.

There were desertions after the founder's death, but the Unity went on. Its extensive land holdings rose in value. It added an electric light plant, a wood-working plant, machine shop, laundry and bakery to the list of its enterprises. A part of its beach land was developed and sold. New adherents were not so easy to get. Six months' probation is required during which the applicant must study and fully accept the Koreshan teachings. Whisky and tobacco are banned. Every applicant must prove his willingness to work. Those entering the community contribute what they have of this earth's goods —little or much—to the general treasury. In turn they receive the support of the combined resources of the Unity. They live quietly and at peace with their neighbors and the world. No member of the Koreshan sect ever burned an obdurate fellow-man at the stake for refusing to accept Dr. Teed's conclusions as to the hollow nature of our allegedly whirling sphere. No howling group of gesticulating Koreshaners ever screamed about a bonfire made of books which do not concur in Dr. Teed's conclusions as to the inherent poison in the competitive system or the advantages of collective ownership. Perhaps tolerance is the key to their modest growth. New causes, they say, need strident screamers; bung-eyed fanatics, thick-necked, thick-waisted and thick-ankled adherents, who ask no reasons why but merely whom to strike and when. The gentleman from Nazareth took the quiet way. Most of His adherents took the other. Today the votes seem to show that the old Human Animal needs the stridency; the hotfoot, the club and the brass knuckles. Perhaps.

CHAPTER 22

SILVER-SIDES AND HAMMERHEADS

ALL Florida is undivided. Down both coasts and off Key West is one vast fishing camp. Few men are brave enough, or well informed enough to join in debate as to whether the East Coast or the West Coast has the better waters for non-commercial sporting fishing. True, the great Gulf Stream brings advantages to the East Coast— the sailfish, the bonito, the amberjack and the dolphin. But most of these are found on the West Coast too, besides, for the early winter fishing, grouper and the sea trout. Great schools of flashing king and Spanish mackerel arrive in the Gulf in March and April and furnish sport unequaled in its class in the world; and then in May and June come the tarpon!

Traditionally along the Mangrove Coast the tarpon season opens May 15th. There is no legal season for tarpon. Great schools of the giant silver-sides commence working north from the waters about Panama Bay and the Mosquito Coast early in January and within the month the first of the tarpon are being caught off the beach of the Cape Sable country and in the broad reaches of the Shark River. But the tournaments, held by almost every community from Tarpon Springs to Everglades City, generally start in mid-May and finish on the first of August. Sarasota claims to have conducted the oldest continuous tarpon tournament in the world but other communities along the coast had organized tarpon fishing contests earlier. Today Boca Grande is the center for early tarpon fishing. From late April to early June splendid tarpon fishing can be found in the deep channel of Boca Grande pass. Five to eight magnificent forty-five to one hundred and fifty pounders have been caught by a single man in a day at Boca Grande in late May, but the law now holds the fishermen to one tarpon per rod per trip. The fishing is good both on the morning and evening tides and the fleet of "charter" boats seen at sunset is unforgettable.

Before the war fishermen came from all over the world to take a fling at the tarpon. British sportsmen made annual excursions to Boca Grande, Venice-Nokomis, Sarasota and Pinellas county beaches; distinguished statesmen, jurists, industrialists and simple fishermen from all over North America made the pilgrimage an annual devotion. The British sportsmen discovered the thrill in a tarpon strike back in the nineteenth century. Forty years ago the Duke of Sutherland in his famous globe-trotting yacht, the *Sans Peur*, every year visited every good tarpon hole along the beach with a deputation of lucky, fish-minded Britishers.

The great fish move north seeking crabs and other marine food. Enormous schools, leaping into the air, threshing the water with their tails, roll their way northward following the contour of the gulf coast. By mid-June most of the tarpon are off the Venice, Sarasota, Clearwater beaches in great schools. By July tarpon can be caught off Mobile. Still another great stream of northward moving tarpon come up from Mexican waters and work along the Texas littoral, the two streams merging off the Louisiana coast.

Until the summer of 1885, it was gospel along the Florida gulf coast that a tarpon could never be caught with ordinary tackle and bait and that if a tarpon tangled on such gear the tackle would break in less than five minutes.

Harpoons were used for tarpon. The Indians liked the heavy, coarse meat of the fish and usually speared them. There were recorded instances where the great silver-sides had been trapped in nets. Some had been caught with a shark outfit of rope and chain. There were no recorded catches with rod and reel.

Every spring the vast schools swept in from the south, leaping clear of the water in wonderful flashes of iridescent silver, rolling with the tide, flipping their tails apparently utterly uninterested in any form of lure. On every hotel porch from Schlutz's at Punta Rassa to the old Bell Haven on Sarasota Bay, the arguments were on how to bring the beauties in. But no one did anything about it until W. H. Wood, a New York City sportsman, experienced with deep sea fishing in the east, came along. Determined to prove that with proper fishing the tarpon could be caught on hook and line, he ordered a special reel. It was a white metal and rubber job that was made to hold twelve hundred feet of twenty-one thread line, without gearing. Two extra strong bamboo poles were constructed, each five feet long. A gaff hook, attached to an ash hoe handle, completed the equipment. Wood chose a codfish hook and, at Punta Rassa, decided to bait the hooks with mullet tied on with wire. Some of the old fishermen who lived at Punta Rassa talked with him and watched him. They were not enthusiastic.

"How you going to hold a sixty-pound tarpon if you get one on a little pole like that?" asked one. "A good tarpon'll give you one flip of his tail and jerk that switch right out of your hands or he'll bust it in two."

"But I'll play him," said Wood. "I'll play him and tire him out. Then he can be brought in and gaffed."

"Sure," said one of the old fellows, "you'll play him. But he'll play you and if you don't watch out he'll jerk you out of the boat and then all the playing will be his'n."

Wood suffered many a jeer from the local fishing colony. Late in March his day arrived, fifty-six years ago.

He was working from a skiff close in shore toward a beach lined with mangroves. He was using mullet for bait. He noted tarpon playing close in, and as his guide moved toward the rolling fish he caught sight of another tarpon fifty feet out. He cast his bait six feet ahead of the tarpon and the big fish whirled and took it. Then his booty trailed off slowly with the bait apparently held lightly in his mouth.

"I gave him fifteen or twenty feet of extra line," said Mr. Wood, thereby establishing himself once and for all as a sound tarpon fisherman, "and I waited until he had taken up all of the slack. When it seemed he had it firmly in his mouth, I drew in sharply and hooked him.

"Instantly the big fish was up and out of the water, gleaming in the sun, and shaking his head to dislodge the hook. We paddled toward him to pick up line and he made off through the water. He must have carried us half a mile and during the run made six other leaps in the air, fighting hard to rid his mouth of the hook. Then he slowed down, and in his next leap hardly cleared water. As he tired I slowly worked him close to the rowboat. I wanted to gaff him but my guide was afraid if we brought him into the boat he would knock it to pieces. So I waited. When a sailboat came along I stepped into it and began reeling him in. It was Mr. Smith who gaffed him finally, then we brought him into our boat. A tarpon had been caught with a twenty-one thread line, on a

five-foot bamboo rod with never more than two hundred
and fifty feet of line out. It could be done! We had taken
only twenty-six and a half minutes to land him."

That was a first. Wood took his fish in good time. Even
with modern tackle and with all the experience in tarpon
fishing that has been piled up in the last half century,
landing a ninety-three-pound tarpon from a rowboat,
with no friendly and powerful engine to help, in twenty-
six and a half minutes is a remarkable performance.

Without realizing it at the time, Wood invented a
new and fascinating sport and initiated a great tourist
attraction. Ten thousand tarpon-fishing tourists, at least,
visit the resorts of the Mangrove Coast every year between May 15th and August 1st. Around three thousand
tarpon are landed yearly, at times more. Tarpon fishing
has become a cult. One man I know has caught one
thousand three hundred and seventy-five tarpon in the
last twenty-five years and hopes to make it fourteen
hundred before his fishing days are over. There seem to
be as many of the great fish as ever but old guides will
tell you that the tarpon are becoming smarter. They take
the lure less easily. On the other hand the tarpon fishermen are no longer so hungry for the kill. Dozens of tarpon are caught each year; their weight estimated, snap-
shots taken and then returned to the sea. The fish have
no value as food, and several of the best tarpon tournaments no longer require the "body" in order to partici-

pate in the awarding of the prizes. The report of the fisherman and his guide are all that is required.

"A man who will fight a tarpon for thirty minutes to an hour and a half and then release him isn't the sort of fellow who would lie about ten or twenty pounds," says one club official, "and a good guide is a reliable estimator of weight. We want the tarpon to live."

Tarpon caught in recent years along the Mangrove Coast have weighed up to two hundred and three pounds. Twenty-five years ago several caught in Sarasota Bay weighed up to two hundred and sixteen pounds but today the tarpon, though often playing in the bay, rarely take the lure except outside in the main body of the gulf. Tarpon seldom show up until May 15th but a few have been caught in upper Sarasota Bay as early as mid-January. Generally speaking, baby tarpon—meaning small tarpon weighing from three to six pounds and every pound a ton of fight—start showing in the Shark River section early in February. From then on the march of the tarpon up the coast depends on the increasing warmth of the water and the behavior of the crabs upon which they feed. The tarpon follow the crabs and the crabs go north according to the heat.

Tarpon fishing is a cross between hunting elephants, searching for whale and picking up a live wire. You do not cast your lure into a likely "spot." There simply isn't such a thing. There are places, like Boca Grande channel,

Mansota beach near Venice or off "the Pines" on Longboat Key where they do seem to gather more certainly
than elsewhere, but by and large, tarpon are where you
find them. The boats go out in the early morning just
before dawn, and, as the sun moves up through the pink
and blue mists, the guides and fishermen eye the horizon
line for signs of fish. Sometimes you will spot them—fifty
or a hundred of them—madly thrashing about in circles,
their tails flashing in the sun like propeller blades, the
water churned foamy. Again you will sight them, slowly
and solemnly marching, two by two in almost equidistant
lines, down some invisible sea lane. You can bring your
boat down between them and often they will not even
sound at your approach. Another time they will roll and
dive about your boat so close you can touch them with
a pole, or a pair of them will start ahead of your boat
and play tag with you for miles without ever stopping
to show the slightest interest in bait. At times when there
will be hundreds of tarpon exploding about you, boiling
up in clusters on all sides, not a fish will be taken.

Then suddenly the fish will bite!

When the biting streak occurs, about once or twice
in twenty-four hours, they all seem to bite at once furiously, recklessly, at almost anything. Then the mood
will seem to pass as suddenly as it started. Between times
there is little to do but wait, and hope. Occasionally there
will be short biting periods at midday. Once in a while a
single tarpon will be caught when the rest of the school

seem to be utterly devoid of any interest in food. That does not happen often. Generally speaking tarpon bite when they bite and they don't when they won't.

The fishing varies slightly in different localities. After a school has been located, the fishing boat, generally a gas driven vessel from twenty to thirty feet in length, fishing two rods, will approach slowly. No great care has to be taken as the fish pay no attention to the boats when they are at play. In the Boca Grande Channel sportsmen usually fish off the bottom, baiting their hooks with crab and keeping around fifteen feet off the floor of the gulf. The boats push along at about two miles an hour dragging the bait and tackle behind them. The strike is invariably light. The fish takes the bait gently into its mouth, as if it were afraid of crushing it, and will run for fifteen or twenty feet with it. The fish will then come down on the bait and then is the time to strike. Hundreds of tarpon are lost every year through a too quick jerk back on the pole. Men who are used to casting for bass, for instance, find it hard to overcome the tendency to pull back wildly when they feel the strike. If they do, almost invariably the tarpon drops the bait and gets away. This explains why freshmen tarpon fisherwomen are often more successful than men. When a man feels a strike he almost always instinctively responds with a quick jerk. Women, on the other hand, will often drop the pole and scream, "I've got a fish, what'll I do?" The tarpon begins to move away and about the time she seizes her rod and swings it back, the tarpon has bitten down on the crab—and she has her fish hooked on her line.

North of Boca Grande it is customary to use a big white and red bobber with about fifteen or eighteen feet of line floating free with the bait. When the tarpon are sighted and a safe approach has been made, the fisherman casts his line in front of the game fish he hopes to attract as they swim past. If the fish are in a biting mood, the move brings success.

The instant the tarpon feels the hook the battle is on. There are few feeble fighters. The big silver-sides will be in the air with a smashing rush, the water will fall away in waves as he comes up, his head shaking madly to throw off the hook. Three—four—five times he will make the leap and then will probably sound deeply and see-saw all the way up. An average weight for tarpon is around sixty-five pounds and a sixty-five pounder can keep a fisherman in a state of nervous hysteria for twenty-five minutes without exerting himself at all. I have seen tarpon fishermen so exhausted after a twenty-five-minute continuous leaping, sawing and jumping match with a tarpon as not to be able to stand or to speak from sheer mental and physical exhaustion for ten minutes. These men only want one tarpon a season.

Some men come to the Mangrove Coast year after year and fail to get their tarpon. Others will average a tarpon a tide for a week at a time. Jesse Tucker, a well-known

Sarasota tarpon fisherman, holds a Mangrove Coast record for catching five tarpon, ranging from fifty-five pounds to one hundred and two pounds, in four hours. But Jesse once hooked a tarpon off a bay bridge, while casting for mackerel, and held it for two jumps before the startled fish was able to run the line out and get away. Lassoing a tarpon is not frequent, but both Kirk Lincoln and V. T. Hamlin, the well-known newspaper cartoonist, have so cast their lines as to have them whip about the flourishing tail of a tarpon and both were able to bring their fish to gaff. A few years ago on a bet Bert Cohn floated out into the gulf in a barrel, made a cast and caught and killed his tarpon—a 125-pounder.

The guides tell you that only ten per cent of any school of tarpon are ever seen on the surface at one time. If the proportion is correct, a school of five hundred tarpon can not be at all unusual, for I have often seen fifty tarpon rolling and tossing at one time.

Even a school of five hundred tarpon the guides will say is no great shucks. From Clearwater to Boca Grande every guide will swear to having seen that many at one time rolling in a long creaming line in the moonlight. That would mean schools of at least five thousand fish.

Once I was out fishing the late afternoon tide. Tarpon fishermen as a rule are a conservative lot and resist innovation, but Oscar Babcock had cut a trap door in the cabin of his new thirty footer, thus enabling Wesley, his guide, to stand on the high steersman's chair, operate the steering wheel with the big toe of his right foot and yet keep an eager eye out for sign of fish.

The sun was slipping into an explosion of turquoise and red clouds and the boat was rising and falling easily with gentle roll. In the tiny galley Archie was working over the stove heating up the soup and the coffee. As he worked he talked.

"Once in a while you will see a school of tarpon a thousand fish or more," said Archie. "I saw a school like that last week almost a quarter of a mile long. And there wasn't a bite in the whole parade."

Wesley came down from his standing perch and resumed his seat at the wheel.

"Best time to see tarpon," he said, "is at night. And the best night is a dark one. A dark night when the phosphorus is burning good. After a shower, in the dark of the moon. The water fires up fine then and you can see the tarpon cutting through the water a hundred yards off. You can see them from head to tail then, looking like they had their insides trimmed with neon signs.

"I was off the 'Pines' north of Sarasota last summer," he went on, "when one night I saw a glow off toward the shore. I brought the boat up within thirty yards of it. You could see plain it was nothing but tarpon. Must have been thousands of them. A glowing line for almost a quarter of a mile down the beach. The streak was a full hundred yards wide. Sometimes the mass would run three and four fish deep. They weren't hitting it up and they didn't seem to be going any place. It took 'em about half an hour to pass me. Once in a while one or two would come to the top and roll, and the drops of water would look like pinwheels sparkling. That was the greatest tarpon show I ever saw."

Offshore there was some sort of disturbance in the water. In the late sunlight a light brown patch could be seen just under the surface of the water. A broad, sharply pointed head came up and swung into the air, almost erect.

"Look at that loggerhead," said Arch. "Now if we had a jig I'd go over and let him have it."

"Can one get in that close to them?"

"Lots of times they are asleep but you can slide up pretty close almost any time. These big loggerheads aren't afraid of anything. You will find them often sloshing about on the surface dead asleep. On a light line they'll give you quite a fight but they aren't worth much. The hawkbill turtle shell sells pretty well sometimes and then again it doesn't. We don't hunt them often. A green turtle will give you a pretty good steak but the brown ones aren't good eating. If you want a real fight in these gulf waters take on a manta ray."

"Isn't that a skate?" asked one of the passengers. "I saw one once that was six feet across."

"Six foot," replied Wesley with polite scorn, "is nothing. We don't bother with six-footers. We take them on when they run fifteen to twenty feet across. The biggest one I ever saw was twenty-five foot across. It weighed three thousand pounds and it dragged the boat, a fishing cruiser as big as this, ten miles before it slowed down. The big manta ray are kings of the gulf. Nothing can touch them. They almost let you run into them before they move. But the instant they feel the harpoon sink into them they drop fifty or sixty feet into the water. Then those big flappers of theirs get to working and they head out to sea. As quick as we land a harpoon into one we always throw the boat into reverse until he gets to going good. When he tires after an hour or so we go into reverse again and start pulling just to keep him from getting any rest. A big ray will fight from six to eight hours. I heard of one once that pulled a boat for seventeen miles before he slowed down. Manta ray is the biggest, wildest game in the whole gulf!"

"I saw a manta ray eating once," said Arch. "Something to look at. All there is to their heads is a couple of big eyes that look like tail lights to an automobile and a mouth as big as a bushel basket. We were laying off Venice looking for tarpon and then suddenly this old chap comes up in the middle of a school of sardines. He opens his mouth and brings his big flippers around and scoops up sardine by the bucketful. I mean it—a regular bucketful at every scoop. We took a shot at him with a .30-.30. It didn't even feaze him. It did scare the sardines and they flipped up their tails and shot off."

Wesley had no fear of the sting ray.

"You will never get stung unless you step on one of them," he said, "and even then the sting isn't anything like as bad as a snake bite. It's painful but not fatal. If they get on your line, cut them loose. That's the simplest way."

"Once in a while we jig for them," said Arch. "We like 'em for shark bait."

It was late in May and the high noonday Florida sun was blazing down with all its power. The flat surface of the gulf had the greasy silver look of molten lead. Forward on the tip of the cabin house, in the shade of the tarpaulin temporarily rigged from the signal mast to the shaft of a club burgee, rested the Skipper. His two "sports" were somnolently drinking beer in the cockpit aft. Trailing behind the transom stern were two tarpon, each well over five feet long, caught on the morning tide.

The glassy surface of the gulf just back of the boat broke suddenly. There was the flash of a tail, a blurred vision of a long white under water streak, a horribly gaping mouth and a great dead eye in a soiled ivory setting. The light line that had held one of the tarpon lay listlessly on the water, merely the head and a foot or so of torn tarpon flesh dragging behind.

The Skipper tumbled to the cat deck and slipped back into the cockpit, spitting out words, good, sound pre-Shakespearean profanity.

"It's that God damned old bastard," he spluttered. "That double nosed white bellied sonofabitch. It's the Old 'Un. He's the meanest, hungriest, cussedest hammerhead in the world. If he's hanging around here we might as well beat it. And if we do beat it we will still be lucky if we can shake him off our stern."

And that's how I met the "Old Un," the blight of the tarpon-fishermen's perfect day, the ruthless raider of the seas, the meanest hammerhead, according to gulf coast tarpon fishermen, that ever lived.

All hammerheads, according to the gulf coast guides, are bastards but the "Old Un" is the worst because he is not only a shark with all the bottomless yen for food that goes with shark nature. He is a hammerhead shark and the smartest hammerhead besides.

There are sand sharks fluttering along the Mangrove Coast any month in the year, timid scavengers of the sea, living easy, raiding the great masses of mullet in the winter months. The sand sharks forage along the bay shore for young and luscious sting ray and even follow the yachts for the bits of meat that come overboard from the galley slops. Once in a blue moon a deep-water fisherman will come in with a barracuda but they are so rarely seen along the beach that word of catching one is something of an event at any fisherman's wharf. But the big shark from the deep and yet warm waters off Mexico and Cuba rarely come north until June. Apparently they follow the big schools of tarpon, and lurking off their flanks, pick up any injured or sickly members of the school that drop away from the main body. With uncanny instinct they have learned to hang about the tarpon fishing cruisers and with one mighty rush cut a hooked tarpon and swallow it in one great gulp, leaving scarcely a bare memento to the fisherman.

There is not one authenticated instance of any shark, hammerhead or leopard, ever killing anyone on the coast. Occasionally, of course, a guide gets a hand sliced from a glancing blow as a shark rushes a tarpon when the guide is pulling it aboard.

"See those scratches," said Arch, displaying the back of his right hand. It was lined with slashes, cut as if made with a razor blade. "I got those last week off Gasparilla Key. I was leaning over the side hauling in a tarpon—a forty-five pounder—when a small leopard which had been hanging around all morning made a dash for the fish. I had only a short reach on the gaff and, as I bent over to swing the fish, gaff and all to one side, my hand was under water. The leopard closed his rush and snapped. His teeth just grazed my hand. I don't think it was snapping at my hand special. Whatever happened to be near the tarpon got hit."

This reminded the Skipper of a fisherman who lived on Panther Key, south of Fort Myers, who had had his leg badly striped one day by a leopard shark in much the same fashion. The man had a very large tarpon tied to a small boat and he thought it would be easier to beach the fish and the boat if he jumped overboard in shallow water and dragged the fish ashore first and then picked up his boat. He went overboard in about six feet of water and a leopard smashed in at the tarpon and caught the side of his leg.

"I don't think any of these gulf sharks are looking out for human beings for food," continued the Skipper, "but I'm not anxious to be around when they are hungry, especially if there's any blood in the water. It's funny how quickly they seem to get the scent of blood. You may be fishing for hours without seeing a shark but if you catch a tarpon and he bleeds some into the water, the chances are their ugly beaks will turn up inside of ten minutes. Once they come around they stick with you all day long."

"Did you ever try shooting them?" I asked.

"Doesn't seem to bother them a bit," he said. "Take that old devil out there, that hammerhead. He's the biggest hammerhead I ever saw. I'll bet he will run over twenty feet long and his hammerheaded nose is six feet across. He's been coming around every summer for years. He's worked out a regular system. He'd rather let you catch his tarpon and then take it off your line than fish for himself. We tried shooting him. We let a tarpon out on a line about ten feet off the side of the boat. As the old fellow came up we let him have it. I know we planted at least six .44 slugs in his head. He never even stopped his rush to give us a blink. We could see they hit him but they made no more impression on him than if they were dabs of putty. Our tarpon weighed over seventy pounds and he took over half of it in one clean bite. He just seemed to waft it down."

"The porpoise have their goat, though," said Arch. "You don't see any old sharks fooling around with a porpoise."

Shark versus porpoise has been a moot question on fishing club porches and among the guides for half a century and more. One school holds that the porpoise can chase away any shark and even that, as soon as a school of porpoise shows up, sharks leave.

The studies made of porpoise life through the facilities offered by the construction of the great tanks for the Marine Studios south of St. Augustine add more to our knowledge than any ever made on porpoises before.

By placing various types of shark in the tanks with the porpoise it was discovered that the sand shark was almost immediately attacked by the porpoise which apparently "ganged" up on the shark, and they chased and butted him all over the tank. Attendants had to remove the shark from the tank to save its life. Later a leopard shark was placed in the tank and the behavior of the porpoise was decidedly different. The porpoise stayed well together and kept a sharp watch on the invader but made no effort to attack him. On the other hand the leopard shark stayed as far out of harm's way as possible. Apparently both sides had a respect for the other's fighting powers and neither cared to open hostilities.

Porpoise schools are a familiar sight along the Mangrove Coast. They follow mullet, upon which they feed, and as they must come to the surface of the water for air every few minutes, their disporting is always an interesting show. They breathe through a small nostril located on the back of the head just above the neck and they come to the surface to expel what air remains in their lungs and take on a fresh supply. The Marine Studio observers believe that porpoises communicate with one another by signals made through this nostril. The sharp whistling noises vary, it is believed, to indicate alarm, food, or signals for play.

"Did you ever hear of a fish holding a wake?" asked Arch. No one had.

"The blackfish do," he said. "I've seen them. Those big blackfish run fifteen to twenty-five feet long and you see them in the summer off Cape Sable. If a blackfish gets sick or hurt the whole school will nuzzle it into the shallows and when it dies the waves will wash it ashore. Then the blackfish will hang around in a big circle all the next day. I saw a wake once when I was commercial fishing off Lossman's River. There must have been fifty blackfish sticking around with the dead one washed on the beach. The next day we went by and they were all gone except for the dead one. It was eighteen feet long."

EPILOGUE

Enough. No book can set down the magic of the Mangrove Coast. Though this one has dealt, in one manner or another, with history, it is no history of the region but a call to the historians to see how rich the past of this coast is. Some scholar would serve his country well by research into the part Florida played in the pre-Columbian world of the Caribbean and the gulf. We need to know more of the trend of Spanish exploration and Spanish aims in the fifty years that followed the discovery.

Just one hundred years ago, in January 1842, Josiah Gates established the first permanent white settlement on the Manatee after three hundred years of intermittent effort by other men. Four flags, the Spanish, the British, the Confederate and the Stars and Stripes have flown over the coast; five, one could say, if one adds the short time when the lilies of France waved over the northwest portion of the gulf coast, but that time hardly counts, for the Spanish disputed it and it faded so soon. And some might count the buccaneering banners of the dim republics of Buenos Ayres and Cartagena, tossing against the high blue sky, in the brief tumult of a pirate reign along the keys.

But the pull of the Mangrove Coast is not its history, for neither the historians nor its own people have laid claim or put great value on its past. Its attractions lie in its intangibles: the gleam of white sand, the softness of southwest winds, pink and turquoise sunsets, and the abiding simplicity of its people.

In some curious way, the coast has managed to retain a simplicity in standards and outlook that seems to date back to the early days of the century or, perhaps, instinctively to reach forward into the decades ahead of us all. The people of the coast are like other Americans—they believe in a chicken in the pot and a car in the garage; they believe in these things for everybody, but if the chicken is tender and the car runs, on the Mangrove Coast they do not bother about the year of the car or its lines or its gadgets. Nobody keeps up with the Joneses.

The old-timers tell a story about Bone Mizell that is a true coast story. Bone's name was Napoleon, so of course everybody called him Bone. He was well over six feet, a big hunk of a man, afraid of no one. He trailed along with the Zibe King outfit back of Arcadia and was the only two-footed critter on the great King ranch who would stand up to Zibe and toss it back as hard as Zibe sent it. As a matter of pride, and as a convenience, Bone always wore a ten-gallon hat. In or out of doors he rarely took it off.

Judge Wall was a strict disciplinarian. One day when his court was in session in Arcadia, Bone yanked open the courtroom door and strode down the center aisle, the ten-gallon hat on his head, his eye on the judge.

"Mizell," rapped out the Judge, "come here. I fine you ten dollars for contempt, coming into this court with your hat on."

Bone stared stonily at the judge for an instant, then reached into his high-cut pants pocket and pulled out a bill.

"Here," he said, tossing the money on the Judge's desk, "take twenty dollars. I walked in with it on, and so am I walking out."

From the first, the Mangrove Coast, besides being hospitable and "agin snobs," saw there was a future in the business of entertaining the tourists who came in trailers. While other communities were passing ordinances forbidding trailers from parking within their city limits, Sarasota, for example, was making model arrangements for laundries and social halls and water and light for as many trailers as wanted to come. It boasts today of the finest municipal trailer camp in the world but other cities press it close. Along the Mangrove Coast too it was early recognized that there was social and economic sense in welcoming the fisherman to the bridges, setting a legal place from which to cast his line, and protecting him from the traffic. Appropriations were generous for fine municipal beaches for all the local inhabitants and all the tourists. There are any number of luxurious and exclusive clubs along the coast, but they strike a minor note. They are extras and do not monopolize the wonders of the shore.

The story of the founding of the John and Mabel Ringling Memorial Art Museum at Sarasota, easily the most comprehensive art collection in the Deep South, is the story, not of a museum, but a movement stimulating fresh creative art. Art colonies sprang up all along the coast, in Tarpon Springs, at Clearwater, St. Petersburg, Tampa, Bradenton and at Fort Myers. Local museums everywhere show the local work.

By mid-December the tourists start rolling in from the Midwest and Ohio, down for Christmas. A month later, the New Yorkers, the rich and leisured, the government and corporation pensioners from Connecticut, Pennsylvania and New England come—come for the same reason as the robins do, to evade the cold and eat, to gather in flocks and chatter in high voice. Down on the coast they say the robins come down to get drunk eating the fermented berry of the cabbage palm and point to them on the ground with their thin little legs in the air, helpless and oblivious. Tourists, of course, never touch the berries of the cabbage palm.

There are many things in the colorful life of the Mangrove Coast that I have not touched upon and that are important. I did speak of art and culture. But I did not mention *bolito*. Yet *bolito* daily affects the lives of more people along the coast than art will ever touch. Thousands each day translate their dreams and hunches into definite figures and play their nickels, dimes and dollars upon the numerals so conceived. Dream of a spider and play 7, 17 or 37. See a snake and drop a dime on 35. Every kitchen has its dream book. Of course it's illegal. Intermittently the breath of the law is hot upon the necks of the operators, but nightly from Key West to Tampa in dozens of "parlors" the little numbered balls are thrown.

Cockfighting like *bolito* is a part of our Cuban and Spanish inheritance. Cockfighting, however, is exclusive. The tense groups of men that gather in some remote hammock to witness the best rooster blood of the coast and the South fight it out in a spray of blood and feathers are definitely careful as to who is invited to see the mains. But thousands of dollars change hands in the bets that are screamed across the pits.

The war has made changes everywhere. On the coast one notes that people ride in buses more, but they move about to the same places. There are no priorities or restrictions yet on sunshine or swimming hours. The aged and infirm, the businessmen who have called it a day, are nearly all of them back, though many have gone out of retirement, busy again in their old shops or clogging the streets of Washington. The youth of the coast has been

swept into the army and navy, but in return the youth of
the nation are flooding back into the great camps and
training centers of Florida. Tons of sweaters and socks
go north each week for the Red Cross and to the British
War Relief, and thousands and thousands of dollars besides. They give along the Mangrove Coast—they give,
not "till it hurts," but from nature and habit and with a
sheer, keen joy in giving.

Everybody along the coast talks aviation: its past, its
future. The great bombers roar into the air from MacDill
Field on their wide and vague patrols. They set men
talking about the little experiment twenty-eight years ago
on New Year's day. Mayor A. C. Pheil of St. Petersburg
paid four hundred dollars then to be the first paid passenger on any commercial air line in the world. His
ticket read from St. Petersburg to Tampa and return.
Tony Janus took on his passenger and nosed his old
Benoist biplane into the air, and brought him down at
the Tampa Sarasota Transportation Company's docks.
It was tremendous. Pheil said that part of the way they
flew at 75 miles an hour. Miss Mae Peabody, of Dubuque,
Iowa, went as first lady passenger, and others took the
regular trip at five dollars a head, but the line didn't last
long. The First World War reached out and got Tony.
The Russians offered him bigger money to fly for the
Czar, and he went away and never came back to the
coast. The great dark ships that hover over Gadsden

Point today could swallow half a dozen of Tony's Benoists, but his was a First, and memorable.

The coast has a future. And because it has a future, its past is doubly worth looking into. One is bound to be grateful to those who have already put what they have discovered into sharable form. More people should know about Mrs. Lillie B. McDuffee's "Lure of the Manatee," a privately printed book with a remarkably detailed and documented story of the settlements along the Manatee from 1842 to 1930. For years she rifled old and forgotten letter files in dusty Florida attics, interviewed pioneers, ransacked newspaper files and official records and put together from these sources the best picture we have of the development of an American community along the Florida frontier. Professor A. J. Harris, of Rollins College, Dr. Mark Boyd, of Florida State Women's College at Tallahassee, Professor John C. Gifford, of Miami University, Watt Marchman, secretary of the Florida State Historical Association at St. Augustine, Caritu D. Corse of the Florida Federal Writers' Project, Jacksonville, Commander C. E. Edge of the United States Coast Guard, St. Petersburg, Captain Dudley Knox, retired, of the Office of Naval Records at Washington, the Marine Library at Newport News, and Essex Institute at Salem, Mass., were all endlessly generous in feeding my own curiosity about the coast, with material and helping me check facts.

The publishers of the Tampa and St. Petersburg newspapers opened their files to me. E. D. Lambright, editor of the "Tampa Tribune," especially, turned up sources for me on Gasparilla, and the kind but harried men and women of room 300 at the New York Public Library, who were never too busy to be helpful to a blundering stranger fumbling in their stacks, all have convinced me that the Mangrove Coast, its future and its past, is full of friendly magic. All who come close to it, who have studied its history or fished along its shores, partake of a fellowship.

INDEX

PHOTOGRAPHS